Hidden in the welter of Christian literature a book occasionally appears on a topic so central, so practically important, so basic and un-gimmicky, but so neglected, that you say to yourself, 'Of course, this is what we have been missing'. *And Then There Were Nine* is such a book. Timely, straightforward, practical, challenging, sensible – and, best of all, health-giving – it is just what we need. David Searle dispels the neurotic fear we Christians seem to have developed about God's law; he helps us to see its real purpose and its practical blessings. Here is a primer for young Christians, a guide to those well on the way, and fibre for the spiritual diet of the mature. I wish everyone in our churches would read it.

Sinclair B. Ferguson
Church of Scotland, Glasgow

David Searle's new work *And Then There Were Nine* on the ten commandments casts a shining and healing light into the darkness and tragedy of our disintegrating relativistic and materialistic culture. Part of our contemporary problem is that many church people cry 'legalism' the moment God's law is mentioned. But none who have read David's work can justly do so, for all that he says is fond love for God and mankind, and flows from the saving grace of God in Christ. He answers with poignant and intriguing detail the question raised by Francis Schaeffer (following Ezekiel) years ago: 'How shall we then live?' He presses home, with clear illustrations from a long and fruitful pastoral experience, the relevance of God's alternative to moral confusion and personal grief. This book is 'a tract for the times'. If even a large minority of the church would put it into practice, I suspect we would see major changes in society. He presents us with a ripe opportunity, for as he says, 'The blacker the sky!, the brighter the star. The more glowering the clouds, the more beautiful the rainbow. The darker the night, the clearer the light to show us the right path.'

Douglas F. Kelly,
Reformed Theological Seminary,
Charlotte, North Carolina

Pastoral and prophetic, clear and convicting, David Searle's gentle survey of God's blockbusting ten commandments overflows with truth and wisdom. I would like to see it made compulsory reading for all church members

J I Packer,
Regent College, Vancouver

And Then There Were Nine

Dedication

For Alaric, Angelika, Chiara and Sean
with the prayer
that the Commandments of God
given in grace
may continue to guide you
into his loving will
which is perfect freedom

And Then There Were Nine

David C. Searle

Christian Focus/
Rutherford House

Christian Focus Publications publishes biblically-accurate books for adults and children. The books in the adult range are published in three imprints.

Christian Heritage contains classic writings from the past.

Christian Focus contains popular works including biographies, commentaries, doctrine, and Christian living.

Mentor focuses on books written at a level suitable for Bible College and seminary students, pastors, and others; the imprint includes commentaries, doctrinal studies, examination of current issues, and church history.

For a free catalogue of all our titles, please write to
Christian Focus Publications,
Geanies House, Fearn,
Ross-shire, IV20 1TW, Great Britain

For details of our titles visit us on our web site
http://www.christianfocus.com

ISBN 1 85792 510 6

Published in 2000
by
Christian Focus Publications, Geanies House, Fearn, Ross-shire, IV20 1TW, Great Britain and by Rutherford House 17 Claremont Park Edinburgh EH6 7PJ

Cover design by Owen Daily

Contents

Acknowledgements

In preparing this little book on the Ten Commandments, I want to acknowledge my immense debt to the three congregations for whom I sought to expound the grace of the divine law: Newhills Parish Church in Aberdeenshire, Larbert Old Church in Stirlingshire, and Hamilton Road Presbyterian Church in Bangor, Northern Ireland. From my people in each of these fellowships I learned much and I am in their debt for all they taught me as they listened and reacted to my sermons in that ongoing dialogue between preacher and people which can be so constructive and productive for God's people.

I also wish to acknowledge three books in particular (in addition to the standard commentaries on Exodus) which I found of great help in my sermon preparation. First, there was the magisterial treatment of the Decalogue by John Calvin. Second, there was the invaluable study of the Ten Commandments by Thomas Watson (republished by Banner of Truth, 1959) – I truly 'struck gold' when I discovered Watson's work. Thirdly, I found much help and contemporary application of Exodus 20 in the study by Fred Catherwood, *First Things First* (Lion, 1979). Readers who are familiar with any of these three works will recognise their influence on my preaching, and hence on this book.

To all of these I offer my grateful thanks.

David C. Searle

9

Introduction to the Ten Commandments
Enjoying the Christian Life

And God spoke all these words: 'I am the LORD your God who brought you out of Egypt, out of the land of slavery' (Exod. 20:1-2).

It is well known that the Church in Korea has made dramatic progress since the first Christian missionary was martyred there in the 1880s. Today, every Korean city has hundreds of churches which are well attended, generously supported, and still growing fast. Indeed, in the past hundred years, the Korean Church has doubled every decade.

During a visit to Korea a few years ago, while I was profoundly impressed by what I saw there of the Church, there was something which distressed me. There is a small movement within the Korean Church advocating that the Lord's Day be used for recreation, sport and personal business left over from the busy week.

The Commandments today

The argument of this movement is simple: *Christ is the end of the law...* (Rom. 10:4) means that the Ten Commandments are abolished and the only 'Law' governing New Testament Christians is the Law of Love (John 15:17, *This is my command: Love each other*). This teaching, alas, was initiated

11

by a Korean who, while studying theology in London, joined one of the many 'fellowship churches' there, and then took the interpretation of 'Law' he learned there back to his own land.

Before we study each of the Ten Commandments in turn, we look first at the introduction to the Commandments given in Exodus 20:1-2.

Common confusion

When one is reading the New Testament, especially passages where the Old Testament Law is being discussed (e.g. Galatians), it is easy to be confused by the writer's method. Paul often puts himself in the shoes of the Jew who is objecting to the Gospel of grace through faith in Christ, and he speaks as if it had once been possible to attain acceptance with God by keeping the Law. But it is important to note that Paul himself never actually says that. Because the Bible nowhere teaches it.

Confusion can also arise unless one understands what Paul means by 'the Law'. Some Christians (like the members of the fellowship church mentioned above) confuse 'the Law' with the Ten Commandments. But usually what is meant by the Law in our New Testament is the whole Old Testament system of worship, with its ceremonial washings, sacrifices, categories of what was clean and unclean, along with the temple and priesthood. We might even say that by 'the Law' Paul means 'religion'. So the first point that must be made in approaching the Ten Commandments is that they are not to be confused (or even equated) with the Law in the New Testament writings.

Distinction made
In the books of Exodus, Leviticus and Deuteronomy, a clear distinction is made on the one hand between the great mass of laws which they contain, and the Ten Commandments which we find in Exodus 20 – and again in Deuteronomy 5. In a very special way, the Ten Commandments are set apart as quite distinct and in a class of their own.

God spoke
There are several differences between the Ten Commandments and the other laws which go to make up the whole Levitical system of daily life and worship. One is that the Ten Commandments were spoken by the mouth of God and written by his finger. All other laws of the entire Levitical system were given by God through Moses as mediator. But the Ten Commandments came direct from God, and the people heard the thunder of his voice (Exod. 19:19; 20:1a, 18f).

Kept in the Ark of the Covenant
Another difference is that of all the many laws given through Moses it was only the Ten Commandments, written on two tablets of stone, which were kept in the Ark of the Covenant. The

Ark itself was in the Holy of Holies, the innermost sanctuary within the Tent of Meeting, into which only the High Priest entered once each year. The Shekinah Glory of God rested on the lid which covered the Ark, giving both the Ark and its precious contents the very highest place in Hebrew thought and worship.

Apodictic absolutes

'Apodictic' means 'clearly established'. This word explains another major difference between the Ten Commandments and all other Levitical laws of Judaism. The other laws are what we call 'case laws'. But the Ten Commandments are absolute laws, clearly established by God, and not open to any kind of change or modification.

I once consulted a lawyer over a rather difficult matter, and he began to look up various legal volumes and quote to me court rulings that had been made in the past in similar cases. Much law is established by 'cases'. Glance at Exodus 21 and the following chapters to see that Levitical law is 'case law' – instructions given for particular situations.

But the Ten Commandments are quite different. They are absolutes, 'apodictic absolutes'. They are commandments spoken by the mouth of God and written by his finger to govern his people's living whatever the circumstances or conditions of the case may be. Given these three major differences between the Ten Commandments and Levitical laws, we can see why we can neither go along with the bad theology the Korean took back home with him, nor disregard any of the Ten Commandments.

If someone asks, 'What then did Paul mean when he says, "Christ is the end of the law"?', the answer is that Christ has both fulfilled the law and brought to an end the Levitical system of sacrificial worship along with all the ritual accompanying it. In fulfilling the law, he has demonstrated clearly that it was all in a very special way prophetic, pointing forward to his Person and Work. Moreover, in his fulfilment of the Levitical system, he renders it redundant as he gathers to himself the office of High Priest, and is himself the sacrifice for sin. But as he himself said, he did not come to abolish the Law but to fulfil it. *Anyone who breaks one of the least of these commandments and teaches others to do the same will be called least in the kingdom of heaven, but whoever practises and teaches these commands will be called great in the kingdom of heaven* (Matt. 5:19).

The Grace of Law

However, the most important point about the Ten Commandments has still to be made. It is that they are grounded in the love of God. God had chosen this ragamuffin band of fugitives from the concentration camps of Egypt. Why, we will never know – except that inexplicably he loved them.

Redemption

More, God entered into direct confrontation with possibly the most powerful man in the world at that time in order to free these slaves from their miserable lives of unremitting toil. He gave the Passover lamb and provided its blood to be sprinkled on each of his people's doorposts and lintels. He parted the Red Sea by his breath. He satisfied the people's hunger by providing a table in the wilderness, and quenched their thirst by water from the rock.

In other words, the Lord was their God. He has loved and redeemed them, so they are his people. The Ten Commandments, therefore, are given in grace. That is why the first two verses of Exodus 20 are so important: *I am the LORD your God, who brought you out of Egypt, out of the land of slavery.* Take this statement away, and we are left with only Law. Leave them in their place, and we have the Grace of Law.

The way of blessing

Properly understood, the Ten Commandments are the pathway of life. *Do this and live* (Lev. 18:5; Deut. 30:11ff), never meant, 'Do this and *earn* life', as the Rabbis erroneously taught. Rather it meant, 'Do this and *enjoy* life' – the life I the Lord have given you.

That is what they mean for us today. The Ten Commandments are not only the absolute commands of God, they are also his gracious invitation to us to follow a path that is safe, good and blessed, a path that leads to heaven. Not that heaven is ever reached *because* we keep these commands; rather that, having been redeemed by Christ our Passover Lamb, having eaten of him our bread from heaven, and having drunk of him the water of life, our feet are now guided to walk the way of his commandments. Therefore, they are the path to glory.

Holiness

Many of us can remember the first exhilaration we experienced when we found Christ as Saviour. The whole world seemed to be transformed, and indeed was transformed. 'Heaven above was softer blue, earth around was deeper green....' Our joy knew no bounds. But after some weeks came the realisation that the Christian life was more than a Vision; it was also a Way. A way has to be trodden, and as one walks, feet can become sore and blistered.

Obedience

I mean that as young Christians we had to learn that followers of the Lord must learn obedience to him. Such obedience is often costly. It demands that we say no to some natural inclinations, even that we die many painful deaths to self. Put another way, this obedience to Christ is nothing less than obeying his commandments. His two great commandments are actually a summary of the Ten

Commandments. 'Love God' sums up the first four; 'Love your neighbour' sums up the remaining six.

It is evident, therefore, that to say any single one of the Ten Commandments no longer applies to Christians is quite false. After justification – the divine act whereby we are acquitted at the judgment bar of God and accepted in Christ as children of God, there comes sanctification – the long, slow process of holiness that takes a whole lifetime and consists in our becoming more and more like the Lord Jesus himself. It is as we obey his commandments through the help of the Spirit of God that we become like our Lord and enter more deeply into the process of sanctification or holiness.

In other words, obedience and likeness to Jesus Christ cannot be separated from the commandments of God. The commandments provide the way of holiness, and without holiness no one will see God.

This little book seeks to explain the Ten Commandments and show their relevance for today. It is because they are so important for Christian living that we will study each commandment in turn.

The
First
Commandment

You shall have no other gods before me
(Exod. 20:3).

You shall love the Lord your God with all your heart and with all your soul, and with all your mind. This is the first and greatest commandment (Matt. 22:37-38).

The essence of true Christianity is to enthrone the Lord God in our lives. To honour, obey and serve Him first of all. Yet how easy in our age of materialism to worship 'other gods' – a home, a sport, a bank-balance, a 'thing'; or perhaps that most secret rival of all to the Lord, 'self'.

Lord, I understand *with my mind* that You are God; that You have filled this teeming world with all its treasures. I know that You have entrusted us with all You have made to enjoy and care for. And I know, Lord, that I am to worship only You, for the gift of Your love is that You should be my God.

Yet, Lord, as I am alone before You, this word of Your first commandment convicts me of my failure. I find uncovered 'other gods' which try to gain first place in my thoughts and affections. I have not enthroned You in my heart, or loved and served You above all else.

The more I ponder Your Word, the more I realise that I have not appreciated the privilege of Your friendship. Blindly and madly, I have run after fleeting fancies. I have raised up idols in my heart which I have adored, and which have absorbed all my efforts day after day. You, Lord, have often been forgotten.

My child, many times I have called you, but you have gone away refusing My voice. I have stood in your pathway, to confront you with My Presence, but you have turned aside. To win you with My love, I have answered your prayers. But you have hurried on, without Me. This is the sin of all mankind, to ignore My Word and spurn My call.

Lord, forgive my sin. Open my eyes anew to see Your glory. Unstop my ears to hear Your voice. Bend my proud will to turn to You truly. Melt my hard heart to receive You humbly.

Child, you call Me LORD. And so I am. I have loved you eternally that you may love Me in return. For I have made you for Myself, and your heart can only find its rest in Me.

The First Commandment
No False Gods

You shall have no other gods before me
(Exod. 20:3).

As a boy, I often puzzled over what the Bible means when it says that man and woman were created 'in the image of God'. One aspect of the meaning must be that humankind is distinct from other living creatures. One of the distinctions between humankind and all other creatures most certainly is that humans have a capacity for spiritual worship which other creatures do not have.

In other words, men and women have been created as worshipping beings. To put it negatively, we all suffer from a 'God-shaped hole in the heart'. Those who know and love the Lord watch with sadness as so many try to fill the empty gap with other gods: sport, ambition, money, possessions, some person, a pastime – the gods we create for ourselves are too numerous to name. We take the gifts of the Creator and worship and serve them rather than the Giver of those wonderful gifts.

Turning to other gods
It is significant that this first commandment was given, not to people who had no knowledge of God, but to those who had been redeemed and had experienced the power and presence of God in the

most remarkable ways. Re-read the early chapters of Exodus to see how God had demonstrated to his people the reality of his being and the greatness of his love. So it was to those who knew him and had witnessed his mighty acts that God gave this commandment that they were to have no other gods before him.

I remember as a student often travelling by the London underground. As I sat, I could look through the window of the door separating my carriage from the next, and it appeared to me that the passengers in the adjoining carriage were having a very rough journey – they were being shaken and rocked about in an alarming manner. Then I realised that half the rocking and shaking was going on in the carriage where I was seated!

Do we get the point? We read the papers and watch the news, and are shocked that people so blatantly worship 'other gods'. What we can miss is that we too turn from the Lord to 'other gods'. What is a 'god' anyway? It is anything that comes first in our lives. It's our number one priority.

Three tests
Try out the following three tests to discover what comes first in your life.

The money test
Jot down the main items of your monthly or annual spending. After you've accounted for the essentials of life such as rent or mortgage, food, heat and

clothing, see how you spend the rest. For example, compare how much you spend on holidays each year with what you give to the Lord's work. Because how we spend our money will tell us very accurately what or who is our 'god'.

The thought test
What is your waking thought, and what your last thought at night? Or if you have a couple of hours alone with yourself, and nothing urgent to do, what do you think about, what do you plan? In other words, what do you worship? We are not what we *think* we are. What we think, *we are*. Our religion is what we do with our solitariness.

The time test
Do the same test on your time as on your money and thought life. See how you allocate spare time, and then collate the results of all three tests, and discover fairly accurately some very personal facts about yourself. Discover the identity of the 'god' enthroned in your life.

Like a journey on the London underground, we can see the faults of others; it is obvious they are bumping and shaking. But we can miss our own faults and fail to see that we are breaking this first commandment every day of our lives.

Turning to the Lord God
Some of us recall those rather tyrannical (and sometimes rather cruel) teachers who became so

exasperated with slow or difficult pupils that they mocked and poked fun at them. But a good teacher will take a very different line. A good teacher will fairly and consistently correct the pupils' errors and show them the right way.

God does not give us this first commandment to mock us, or even to scold us. We have already seen that he begins by saying, *I am the Lord your God who brought you out of the land of slavery.* In other words, 'I have redeemed you and loved you, chosen you and called you. I am your God. That is why you shall have no other gods before me.'

An unmistakable call

The word *you* is singular in Hebrew. The commandment is not a general statement. It is a personal word to each one of us as individuals.

I was once called to a home where the young husband was fast becoming an alcoholic. Every night of the week he was in the pub drinking himself senseless. His wife had given him an ultimatum: 'You will have to choose between alcohol and me. I will be a faithful wife to you if you want me. But you can't have me and come home dead drunk seven nights a week. Make up your mind.'

We understand that language, don't we? God speaks to us in language just as plain. 'I will brook no rivals. I must be the only God in your life. You must turn wholly to me. If I am to be your God, you shall have no other gods before me.'

25

In other words, being a Christian means God will accept only our all. He will not put up with playing second fiddle. He will not allow us to offer him the fag-end of our love. He summons us to turn to him, to make him our Lord, without any rival.

The way of happiness
Go back for a moment to that unhappy wife whose husband was proving to be such a waster. I recall another young wife, far from home, living among people whose language she didn't know, whose culture was foreign to her and who was almost completely alone. Her husband's work was demanding and she rarely saw him. She had visited the country on holiday, had fallen in love with a young man who spoke only a few broken words of English and had married him. Now she was realising the rashness of what she had done.

Some of us think that when God commands us to worship him alone, it is a little bit like being an unhappy wife, far from family and friends. We think it is much the same as forsaking everything we know and understand, as we plunge ourselves into a life for which we are unsuited and which will be quite alien to us.

How completely wrong we are. God has created us. He knows us far better than we know ourselves. He knows that we all have a 'God-shaped hole' in our hearts which only he can fill.

Our Maker

The story is told how in the early 20s a motorist on a lonely country road was stuck with a small Ford car which inexplicably had spluttered to a standstill. Knowing nothing about engines, the motorist was at a loss what to do, and was cursing his luck when another car approached and stopped. The driver was most helpful. He lifted the bonnet, and in two minutes had the engine running smoothly. 'How did you manage that?' gasped the delighted motorist. 'Easy', came the answer, 'I designed that car – I'm Henry Ford.'

God designed us. We forget that to our loss. He is our Maker. So when the Maker says, 'Have no other gods before me', it is wisest to listen and obey him. His gracious purpose for us is that we should not only come to know and love him, but also enjoy him. Many people would think it impossible ever to *enjoy* the Lord! Yet that is why he created us, and you and I will only enjoy him when we have no other gods before him. We do well to obey him, for after all his great concern is for our well-being and happiness. Some of us take some convincing of that. We are quick to believe that he is a harsh, unloving father, deliberately trying to spoil our happiness. What a travesty of the truth!

Our Redeemer

Not only is the Lord our Maker, he is also our Redeemer. This first commandment is the beginning of the generous terms he freely offers to those he has ransomed from sin and death. He is unfolding his covenant of grace. The 'glue' of the covenant – on both sides, his and ours – is 'hesed', a Hebrew word which means 'covenant love'. This covenant love is only ever on our side because first it is on his. 'We love him because he first loved us' (1 John 4:19).

True, there is the dimension of holy fear and dread for our God speaks from the fires of Sinai. It is only right that we who are frail, fallen mortals should fear the holy and eternal One. We can be so presumptuous, headstrong, arrogant. We need to tremble before the Lord who is a consuming fire.

Nevertheless, our holy fear of God must be tempered by love for him. This fear and love come together mysteriously and marvellously in the Cross of Christ. For as we draw near to Calvary, the sun is darkened, the earth quakes and the suffering Saviour cries out in agony, 'My God, my God, why have you forsaken me?' Yet our awe before the horror of the crucifixion is tempered by the love that streams from the face of the dying Jesus and from the glory of the smile of the risen Lord.

Therefore as we listen to the commandments of our God, it is only right that awe of him is tempered by love for him. He says, 'I have freed you from your chains of slavery. I have forgiven you. I have redeemed you. I have loved and chosen you. Now, you must have no other gods before me. My purposes for you are for your happiness and security. I want only the best for you. I long that you and I should be friends to enjoy each other for ever.'

Do we enjoy God? Not if someone or something has seized his throne in our lives. Nor if we have secret gods whom we serve and to whom we give our affection and loyalty. Those who 'two-time' their God make the most miserable and dishonourable Christians in the world!

Enjoyment of him is his chief end for his children, for when we enjoy him we glorify him. Then the relationship between us and the Lord will become as it should be, the tenderest, closest, dearest relationship in all the world. The first step towards this highest, most glorious enjoyment of Jesus Christ is to have no other gods before him!

The
Second
Commandment

You shall not make a graven image for yourself
(Exod. 20:4).

They exchanged the truth about God for a lie, and worshipped and served the creature rather than the Creator, who is blessed forever, Amen (Rom. 1:25).

The first commandment is about worshipping false gods; the second commandment is about worshipping the true God in a false way. One of the great failings of us all is to worship the gifts, and to neglect the Giver.

Lord, today I paused to admire a flower. Its beauty struck me with a new realisation of its wonder – the delicacy of its petals, the fragrance of its nectar, the loveliness of its colours. It set me thinking what a world we live in. The rolling mountains and fertile valleys, the peaty burns and majestic rivers ... the grace of birds and the intricacy of tiny things like the honey bee....

And now, Lord, Your Word has come to me that mankind has worshipped and served the creature rather than You, the Creator. I see with shame that I am included in this sin. I loved Your gifts more than I loved You, the Giver. I have struggled to possess what You have made rather than to possess

32

You, the Maker. I have spent years pursuing life, but I have not pursued You who are the Life. I, too, have failed to keep this second commandment, Lord.

My child, this is the way of men and women. They devote themselves to all I have made, to explore with minds that I have given, to appreciate with senses that I have bestowed. My will was that their work should bring them to find in My creation the mirror of My majesty. But instead of finding Me, they have found only My work; and the things I have made they have exalted, without exalting Me.

The sorrow of this world is that, without Me, My gifts can never satisfy the cravings of men's hearts, nor bring the peace for which they search. For this is My way; first you must acknowledge Me, love Me, and serve Me; then you will find My gifts are but My servants to bring you to me.

Lord, I am seeing more clearly that every good and perfect gift is from above, coming down from the Father. May I, in everything, give thanks to you, and be brought closer to You through Your gifts to me.

The Second Commandment
True and False Worship

You shall not make for yourself an idol in the form of anything in heaven above or on the earth beneath or in the waters below. You shall not bow down to them or worship them...
(Exod. 20:4-6).

Have you ever wondered what the difference is between the first and second commandments? It may interest you (if you don't already know) that the Roman Catholic Church merges the first two commandments into one. That may be why Roman Catholics are comfortable with images and icons in their church buildings. Of course, any informed Catholic will assure you that such images are not worshipped, but only used as an 'aid to devotion'.

Roman Catholics draw a distinction between 'worship' and 'veneration'. So a moment's reflection will make it clear that if the first two commandments are treated as one single commandment, it is possible to argue that only images and pictures of *false gods* are forbidden.

'But wait a minute', someone says. 'If the first two commandments are merged into one, that only leaves nine commandments when there should be ten.' The problem can be easily solved, for Roman Catholics divide the tenth commandment into two, and in this way complete the tally of ten. They make the ninth commandment, *You shall not covet your neighbour's house.* And the tenth becomes, *You shall not covet your neighbour's wife...*

The first two commandments

In the Reformed Churches, we follow the traditional Jewish view, as represented by Philo and Josephus, that the second commandment begins at verse 4, *You shall not make for yourself an idol* etc. But if the second commandment begins at verse 4, what is the difference between the first two commandments? The answer must be, *You shall have no other gods before me* (v. 3) forbids the worship of **false gods**. The Lord has said that he, and he alone, is to be the only God in the lives of his people. Whereas, *You shall not make for yourself an idol* etc. (v. 4) forbids **false worship** of the one true God. The Lord is saying in the second commandment that false worship of himself is forbidden, having forbidden worship of false gods in the first commandment.

Ingenious idolatry

The temptation has always been to reduce God to an understandable size. If only we could bring the Almighty to acceptable proportions and define and comprehend him! The earliest attempts to do this resulted in idols carved out of wood or stone. How ridiculous to try and contract the mighty God to proportions that may be contained within the four walls of some temple. He inhabits eternity and fills

35

all creation with his glory!

In our day, we are witnessing fresh attempts to reduce God to a size acceptable to our finite minds. Certain theologians (including bishops of the church) have sought to define God in such a way that there is no mystery, no awesome 'otherness', no transcendent power. They deny the Eternal has broken into time and space and become one of us, or was conceived of the Holy Spirit in the womb of a woman. They deny that he was raised from death by the glory of the Father.

What are we left with? I sometimes wonder if such attempts to make God acceptable to the finite mind don't leave us with a very ordinary Wizard of Oz, a loveable, endearing sort of person, who is behind the scenes pulling handles and twiddling knobs, trying to make the best of rather a bad job, but not doing very well.

Worshipping the creation
The second commandment goes on to say: *You shall not make for yourself an idol in the form of anything in heaven above or on the earth beneath or in the waters below.* Paul restates 'this apodictic absolute' in a slightly different way when he writes that humankind *exchanged the truth of God for a lie, and worshipped and served created things rather than the Creator – who is forever praised* (Rom. 1:25).

The feminists deplore beauty contests, Miss United Kingdom, Miss World and the like. These exhibitions of women (the feminists call them *'exploitations* of women') come dangerously near to violating the second commandment. For a kind of praise is being given to what God has created, as people honour the creature rather than the Creator.

Sex-cult

Today we have the modern sex-cult with its gods and goddesses. Trappings of worship are fashioned around sex. But as with any worship of the creature, it fails to deliver what is longed for, and so new rituals and greater frenzies are devised. The deification of sex is not just absurd, it is destructive, for the tenderest and most sensitive human instincts are ravaged and tortured until they are dead. In the endless search for yet more exciting 'kicks', when the pleasures of sex have been exhausted, there follows abuse of drugs. Inevitably, addiction is the result and that goes on to destroy both mind and body. Such is the consequence of worshipping the creature instead of the Creator.

Church buildings

Many readers will have visited some of the great mediaeval cathedrals, either in our own land or on the continent. You will have admired their grandeur and breathtaking beauty. Then those of you who are Presbyterians have returned to your home churches and to your plain Meeting Houses and found yourselves asking the question why your places of worship are so demure and (compared to the mighty cathedrals) dull.

No, it's not that our forefathers were not clever enough or imaginative enough to build anything better than simple barn churches. Those who founded the Reformed Churches actually preferred plain buildings. They were guided by this second commandment. They saw that too much craftsmanship, too much elaborate art, too much flamboyant decoration could all detract from spiritual worship of God.

So they built Meeting Houses which were beautiful in their chaste plainness. They wrote Psalm music that was appealing in its simplicity. They used their craftsmanship in such a way that it never intruded into the worship. They designed churches that would not offer any distraction from the true worship of God. Their watchword was that *God is a Spirit, and those who worship him must worship Him in spirit and in truth.*

That is not in any way to criticise the magnificent architecture of many fine places of worship. There is a viewpoint which recognises that church buildings may properly give the opportunity for men and women to offer their very best skills to God. The beauty of stone and wood carving, the breathtaking stained-glass, the lofty magnificence of the architecture, the thunder of the great organ – all these are intended to glorify God. Nevertheless, the early Presbyterians, while recognising such worthy motives in the design and structure of the cathedrals, chose simplicity, deliberately suspecting worshippers could be too easily distracted from their focus on God and diverted instead to think about the cleverness of mere men.

True worship

In worship, everything – whatever our denominational affiliation and our opinions on design of church buildings – must point to God. Our psalms and hymns and spiritual songs, the prayers, the readings from Scripture, the sermon, all must be guiding and directing us inexorably in our thoughts and desires towards our God. We must be careful with the many contemporary explorations into new forms of worship and use of orchestras and musical *ensembles* that those who provide such a lead do not intrude into, or distract from, the One before whom we prostrate ourselves in our spiritual worship. Alas, idolatry can rear its head in the most unexpected places and assume the most unlikely shapes!

Giving our allegiance to God

Someone may ask what the word *worship* actually means. Why does the second commandment use two words, *bow down ... worship*? If you look up the Authorised Version, you will see that there *worship* is translated as *serve*. One of the main Hebrew words for worship has the basic meaning of *serve* in the sense of giving one's whole allegiance to a master or a king, and pledging oneself therefore to serve that master all one's days. That is the word used here. God looks for our total allegiance. He asks us to be his bond-slaves all our days and to signify that by bowing before him in adoration and submission. Hence the reason for the two words used in the commandment.

Gratitude
In the final analysis, that kind of worship can only flow from love. Love, in turn, flows from gratitude. Who loves most? The one who is forgiven most. The other side of the coin is that the one who has been forgiven little loves little. This is why the commandments begin as they do, with the mighty statement that God has redeemed his people. *Let the redeemed of the Lord say so.* True worship is when we acknowledge God's marvellous grace by bowing before him in praise, and gladly yielding him our hearts to love and serve him all our days.

The jealousy of God

...for I, the LORD your God, am a jealous God, punishing the children for the sin of the fathers to the third and fourth generation of those who hate me, but showing love to a thousand generations of those who love me and keep my commandments.

There is a tendency today to think of jealousy as silly and immature. But that is not necessarily so.

Jealousy is by no means always wrong. Indeed, jealousy can be very, very right. Certain relationships are meant to be exclusive and shared with no one else. Why else should the Anglican marriage service have the phrase in it, 'forsaking all other'? That is the absolute principle being laid down here. God's jealousy speaks of the exclusiveness of God's love.

Let me illustrate what I mean. I recall reading in the newspapers some years ago of a case which disgusted me. A married couple had been convicted of some crime, but what had come out in the court proceedings had been the basis of their business partnership: the husband had been living off his wife's earnings as a prostitute, and he himself was the pimp who secured for her high-paying customers. Do we not all instinctively feel that kind of an arrangement to be contemptuous? To use a wife like that is surely quite dreadful. We know in our hearts that such a marriage relationship is despicable because the husband-wife love should be exclusive. In the same way, our relationship to God must have an exclusive dimension to it. It is that dimension God himself asks for, and when we deny it to him, his jealousy grieves over our unfaithfulness. Indeed, the Scriptures often depict God as grieving deeply over his people's infidelity as they give their love to other things, adoring the gifts instead of the Giver.

41

The love of God

What has emerged so far in the Ten Commandments is that God is the rightful Lover of his people. The commandments are founded and grounded on his love. Exodus 20:2 makes that clear: *I am the LORD your God who brought you out of Egypt, out of the land of slavery.* He has redeemed these ragamuffin slaves. He is bringing them into a land flowing with milk and honey. He declares himself to be their Lord and God. Now, in the second commandment, his people are being asked to apply their minds to the question of worship. We who are the people of God are to ask why God demands that we worship him exclusively, rightly and truly. The answer is, *for I, the LORD your God, am a jealous God.* And that must mean that the Lord is our rightful Lover.

For us who live under the New Covenant, clearly the issue is how we worship our Saviour. God does not change. His love for his people is still an exclusive love. Are we unfaithful to him, 'two-timing' him and giving our love and worship to the very gifts he has lovingly shared with us instead of exclusively to him? We must learn that our Lord is jealous in his love, and that his Spirit strives over those he loves with an intense and holy envy (James 4:5).

The sins of the fathers

How often have we heard strong objections to the words that come next in the second commandment?

Many people blame this statement for their refusal to believe in the God revealed in the Scriptures. *I am a jealous God, punishing the children for the sins of the fathers to the third and fourth generation of those who hate me....*

Crooked

The AV translates *sins* by the old word *iniquity*. The Hebrew word which used to be translated 'iniquity' has the meaning of being 'twisted' or 'crooked'. In the context of the jealous love of God, the word must mean a particularly despicable form of infidelity. It is not just a 'falling short' in our love for God; rather is it a perverse and perfidious turning from his gracious offer of love to some other utterly unworthy alternative. Hence the phrase *those who hate me*.

But with God, love and mercy go hand in hand. They are the closest of sisters. So when men and women put themselves outside the love of God, they also put themselves outside the mercy of God. Such people enter a land of desolation and despair, a cruel Arctic region where there is no life, no love, no sun, no warmth, no song of birds or hum of bees, but where the cold, jagged ice peaks rise in terrible condemnation of all who turn their backs on those warm and temperate climes where the sunshine of God's love bathes everything in its warm, golden light.

Punishing the children

There are several points that must be made about the statement that the iniquity of the fathers is visited on the children to the third and fourth generations. *First,* this is not God's word to the children. God has his own offer of grace to the children. Rather is it God's word to the parents. It is directed to them to restrain the mad folly of fathers and mothers who are tempted to sin without counting the cost of the effect of *iniquity* on their families. Surely, this is a word of warning urgently needed today!

Second, God never punishes anyone for the sins of another. Ezekiel tells us: *The soul who sins is the one who will die. The son will not share the guilt of the father, nor will the father share the guilt of the son* (18:20). We must not fall into the error of thinking the second commandment is saying the children will bear the guilt of their parents.

Third, the meaning must be that where children imitate their parents (and too often we forget or ignore how much children learn from their parents), God will bring down his righteous punishment upon them, even though they are only doing what they have been taught to do by those divinely ordained to teach them. But they are nonetheless punished for their own sins, even sins taught by, and learned from, parents.

Fourth, there is also the consideration that the 'Land' is closely bound up with God's dealing with his people in Old Testament time. Often part of

God's chastening of his people because of their infidelity to him involved depriving them for several generations of their share in the Land. When that happened, clearly the children had to live with the consequences of their parents' sins.

Let us not, as many have sought to do, try to bring a charge of unrighteousness against God on the grounds of this terrible warning. We do not fully understand how deeply the sins of parents scar the souls of their children. We try to tell ourselves that our peccadilloes hurt no one, do no harm, are our business and no one else's. But no sin is ever private. All sin has a 'domino effect', nowhere else more powerfully than within the family. This commandment gives a solemn warning to those who play fast and loose with God's offer of grace, and end up rejecting and hating the Lord.

Love to a thousand generations
Here is the word for which we sigh and long: the word of overflowing grace. Because although we will never understand the mystery of the one who loves us, yet his purpose is that we should come to know and enjoy him forever. The steadfast love promised here has already been amply illustrated in the earlier chapters of Exodus.

He gives us our daily bread. He supplies that table in the wilderness – the bread that speaks of Christ. He gives us water from the rock, spiritual drink from the Rock cleft for us, which becomes a spring of water within us bubbling up to eternal life. He is a shield around us, and a fiery pillar of cloud before and behind, leading and guiding us through life's perplexing ways. He restrains us from doing wrong, for without his restraining hand you and I would often have made shipwreck of our faith.

Above all, he forgives us. Again and again and again he forgives us. Costly, priceless pardon we could never deserve is lavished on us. This is our God. These are the promises of this second commandment, that he will be our God for a thousand generations, which can only mean forever!

The
Third
Commandment

*You shall not take the Name of the Lord
your God in vain* (Exod. 20:7).

*God has highly exalted Him, and given Him a Name
which is above every name ... Jesus is Lord* (Phil.
2:9-11).

**In days gone by, 'In the King's Name!' meant
'By authority of the king'. To ignore or disobey
a proclamation made in the King's Name was
treason. In other words, the name stood for the
person. So with our God. Reverence for His
Name means reverence for Him.**

Lord, on Sunday in Church, I enjoyed the singing.
Especially one hymn. It was one of my favourites.
The tune was catchy, the organ majestic. I really
'let go'. We all did. When we sat down, I didn't
close my hymn book. I let my eye run over the
words we had been singing:

'At the Name of Jesus, every knee shall bow,
Every tongue confess Him King of glory now ....'

It suddenly struck me, Lord, how far we are from
that. I thought of so many of my friends who don't
know You as Lord. I couldn't help thinking of the
way in which Your holy Name is used as a swear
word – on the bus, in the office, at the club. I found
myself saddened that Your great Name is

in the words, 'In the king's name'. That took in far more than the reigning monarch's actual name. It included honour for the king's laws, the king's officers, the king's rights, as well as honour for the king's person. 'In the king's name' was an expression which carried with it the whole authority, mind and will of the monarch, whoever he happened to be.

So it is here. *The name of the Lord your God* refers to far more than the many biblical names for him. It refers to God himself, to very God. We make a grave mistake if we think we obey this third commandment by simply reverencing the names of God – though that we ought to do! Let's look further at this, and take reverence for the Lord under the three headings of Father, Son and Holy Spirit.

Reverence for the Father
We must begin with the name of God. For though as we have seen the commandment means far more than reverence for his name, that cannot be ignored.

Respect for his name
I wonder if you share with me a sense of acute pain and hurt when God's name is taken in vain. People constantly use the name of God or of the Lord Jesus in much the same way as they might say, 'Bother!' or 'How awful!' I have even heard professing Christians say, 'Good Lord!' as an expression of surprise or disgust. We hear it far too often on radio and television. Every day, this

third commandment is violated, and the blessed name of our God is profaned.

Some argue that it is just a bad habit. But it is more than that. This everyday, common blasphemy has much deeper roots. It shows that the person who profanes the Lord's name is far from God. Because if God was a dear friend then his name would never be misused like that. If he were a tender Father, with whom we often spoke, one whom we deeply loved, then we would never use his name as a common oath.

So the first charge of guilt this commandment levels at those who lightly, easily and unthinkingly misuse his name is this: 'You have not yet come to *know* the Father, far less to *love* him. To you he is only a name, nothing more. When you use his name as an oath, or an expression of surprise, you are telling the world that you are still a stranger to the Lord, still a long way off, distant and remote from him.'

Those who misuse the name are prodigals in the far-off country, and have not found their way home, still have not yet known his arms thrown around them, or been embraced by the Father receiving back those who were lost and are now found.

A first act of treason

We must move on. To use God's name as a common oath also shows that the 'opposition' still has a foothold in our lives. It is basically a blow against God when his name is blasphemed. It is the first act of treason. It is the seed of disobedience. It is the little spark that sets alight the tinder of rebellion.

It does not come originally from *our* hearts to use the name of the Lord as an expletive or a curse. It has a much more sinister source. I wonder if you know the passage in *Pilgrim's Progress* where Christian is passing through the Valley of the Shadow of Death? He goes close by the mouth of hell:

> I took notice that now poor Christian was so confounded, that he did not know his own voice; and thus I perceived it. Just when he was come over against the mouth of the burning pit, one of the wicked ones got behind him, and crept up softly to him; and whisperingly suggested many grievous blasphemies to him – which he truly thought proceeded from his own mind.

Bunyan is so right. The curse against God comes from hell. And when people give their mouths over to incessant curses against God, they have given their hearts over to the enemy of God. Is that not terrible, even frightening? James in his letter in the New Testament writes about people who on the Lord's Day have been praising God, yet later in the week the same lips are cursing God. 'Just a bad habit!' someone says. 'Done without meaning any harm', says someone else. But nonetheless dangerous, nonetheless hellish, for all that. *You shall not misuse the name of the Lord your God, for the Lord will not hold anyone guiltless who misuses His name.*

Outward obedience – inward disobedience
Consider another point. It is clearly possible to have a superficial respect for the name of God. This has been so often the sin of God's people, going right back to Old Testament days. When the Jewish scribes were copying the Scriptures, whenever they came to the name of God in the text, they always took up a new quill. Never would they write any name of God with a quill that had been used already. So that here, in this third commandment, two new quills would be needed.

For all that, the charge that was brought so often against them was this: *You worship God with your lips, but your hearts are far from him.* What use is it if we come to God's House, and we honour him with our lips, we praise him in our psalms and hymns, and then go out from our place of worship to disobey him in our daily living?

We can, therefore, take his name in vain and misuse his name in this way also by appearing to praise him in what we say or sing, when the truth is that we are not honouring him by what we are. We bow our heads in prayer, but our thoughts are miles away; we stand and praise his glorious name, but we are no nearer to God than we are to the moon. As Shakespeare puts it in *Hamlet*:

My words fly up, my thoughts remain below;
words without thoughts never to heaven go!

Perhaps since we attended church last Sunday, some readers have already taken God's name in vain. Perhaps some have already violated this third commandment because, while taking his name on your lips, you have not drawn near to God at all. Your presence among the Lord's people on his Day is nothing more than a mockery, a farce, an empty, meaningless show. Could that be true of some who attend worship regularly? Worshipping with the lips, but all the while far, far away from the waiting Father, who is looking for the prodigal to come home!

Reverence for the Son
The New Testament speaks about profaning Christ. *How much more severely do you think a man deserves to be punished who has trampled the Son of God underfoot, who has treated as an unholy thing the blood of the covenant...* (Heb. 10:29). What is the writer saying?

Coming close
In the communion service, when the Lord's people partake of bread and wine, God sets forth, in a visual as well as spoken form, his Son as the atonement for our sins, the covering for all our guilt. The cup we bless and then drink sets forth an offer of grace and mercy bought by his death on

Calvary. When someone comes very close to the Lord Jesus, so close that they hear and understand this loving offer of mercy – more, they eat the bread and drink the cup – but then turns away from Christ (not, note, to go back into the world but) to seek some other way of salvation, that person then tramples the Son of God underfoot and treats as an unholy thing his blood.

The Lord Jesus told a story which illustrates exactly this point. In the Lord's day, when guests were invited to a wedding, they were given a wedding robe, if they didn't already have one, as they entered the feast. Some of us have experienced a similar custom visiting mosques in Jerusalem or elsewhere. If you are not appropriately dressed with shoulders and arms covered, the Muslim attendant will give you a robe to wear before you may enter.

In the story, the host was speaking with the guests invited to his son's wedding. But then he came to a guest who was not wearing the customary wedding robe. A robe would have been offered at the door to all coming without one, but this guest had apparently declined the offered robe. So he was put out of the feast. He had insulted his host and also his host's son who was being married.

Here is the meaning of that parable. Often we have come near to the cross. We have even taken in our mouths the bread and the wine which speak to our hearts of the new covenant of God's free mercy offered to us in Christ. Yet some turn away from that offered mercy. They are wise in their own conceit. They decide they are good enough as they are. They do not need to repent of sin, and come in humility to Christ. They do not need God's grace in the Lord Jesus. Such an attitude is trampling the Son of God underfoot, and treating as an unholy thing Christ's blood.

No need of repentance

I remember visiting a woman whose husband was dying in hospital. We talked about him and his illness, and I tried to offer her some comfort. As she had no car I offered her a lift to the hospital which was about twelve miles from where she lived. I said, 'I'm going to see your husband myself this afternoon.' Here is what she immediately said: 'Don't you try to pray with him. My husband is not a sinner who needs to repent on his deathbed. He is as good as anyone else. So don't come the religious stuff with him.' It transpired that she was not speaking for him at all, for he was deeply grateful when I read the Bible and prayed with him. His wife was actually speaking for herself.

We can think just as she thought. To put it as plainly and bluntly as I can: we trample the Son of God underfoot, treat as an unholy thing his blood, and crucify him afresh when we shake our heads and say, 'No, I am not a sinner who needs to turn to Christ. I need no forgiveness. I am not a prodigal coming in rags humbly to ask for grace. I am good enough as I am, thank you. None of that for me.'

I have often heard people say: 'I know it all. I

was brought up in the Boys' Brigade, in the Girls' Brigade. I've heard it all. We had to go to church twice on a Sunday. I know the Bible. I got prizes for full attendance at Bible Class. But you will not get me to change. I will take a chance as I am, thank you.'

Well, God alone is the Judge. God alone knows if a man or woman is despising the sacrifice of Christ for sin. That solemn tenth chapter of Hebrews ends with these words: *If anyone shrinks back, I have no pleasure in him.* Then comes this final sentence, which I love: *But we are not of those who shrink back and are destroyed, but of those who believe and are saved.*

Reverence for the Holy Spirit

On one occasion, I was visiting in a psychiatric ward, and I was interrupted by a patient I did not know, and who was not a member of my congregation. He asked if I would have a word with him before I left. So I did. His story was that he had committed the unpardonable sin and was therefore eternally damned. I have to say that after a few minutes' conversation with him, my conclusion was that he was mentally sick rather than unsaved. Such was his sickness that he was sure there was no forgiveness for him. He seemed to be afflicted with a form of religious paranoia, and he had such a low self-esteem that it seemed impossible to tell him God's offer of grace included him too.

The unpardonable sin

What is the unpardonable sin? The Lord explicitly states that blasphemy against the Father and against the Son may be forgiven, but blasphemy against the Holy Spirit cannot ever be forgiven (Mark 3:28f). What is the meaning of that terrible statement?

The Saviour was doing a remarkable work in Galilee. Crowds from a wide area were flocking to hear him teach the word. Lives were being changed. The sick were being healed. There is evidence that during the lifetime of the Lord Jesus, Satan was unusually busy, and had taken possession of many people as a counter-attack on the Lord's great campaign of grace and mercy. But Christ was rescuing those whose lives Satan had seized, and was making them whole again.

Clearly, the religious authorities had to make up their minds about this amazing person and his work. So a delegation of theologians came from Jerusalem to watch and examine the work he was doing. They found themselves caught on the horns of a dilemma. If they admitted his work was of God, then they would have to put themselves under the authority of his preaching. That they were too proud to do. On the other hand, they could not deny the healings and exorcisms. So their verdict was that the power by which Christ was working was the power of Satan.

Christ's reply was infinitely solemn. In effect, he said, 'I am doing my Father's work by the power of the Holy Spirit. You men have attributed the work of the Holy Spirit to the devil. That is a sin which is unpardonable, for you are declaring the divine to be satanic. There is no forgiveness for that. You have hardened your hearts irrevocably against the voice of the Spirit.'

These men were swearing white was black. They saw God at work and said, 'Look at Satan.' They saw the power of the Holy Spirit and said, 'That is the power of hell.' They saw a grace and love which could have changed their hearts and made them different men, and they called that grace evil and that love wickedness. Consequently, they set themselves against God forever; they turned their backs on him; they shut their hearts to him; they closed their eyes that they might never see him.

Dangerously close
Some of us might think such a sin could never be sinned today. However, I have to say that many who attend a place of worship come terribly close to this third and final violation of the commandment, blasphemy against the Holy Spirit. Let me tell you how it can happen.

We see God blessing his work perhaps in our own congregation or maybe elsewhere in some other place. The blessing is by the power of the Spirit in answer to believing prayer. Yet some ascribe that blessing to the work of mere man. Instead of giving glory to God, and acknowledging this is his work, some are blind to his power, and search for the answer in some other explanation. God help us! I know we are not saying that the work is the work of Satan – that *would* be the unpardonable sin. But we are coming too close to that sin for comfort.

I have seen it so often. Someone becomes a Christian – a glorious, old-fashioned, genuine Biblical conversion. What are the comments we hear? 'A passing phase!' Or, 'That minister is having a bad effect on you!' Or, 'Get that nonsense out of your head!' How very dangerous. How perilously near to calling white black! How close to seeing God at work and shutting our eyes to his power, our hearts to his grace!

Conclusion

The third commandment, then, means reverence for the Lord's names. It also means reverence for God as God: Father, Son and Holy Spirit. We live in a cynical age, an age of biting satire, when everyone in authority from Her Majesty, the Prime Minister, the Archbishop of Canterbury and right down to the local petty dignitaries is fair game for ridicule and mockery. How easy to treat the Lord lightly as well.

Pray for God's people. Pray for our nation. Pray that God's holiness may be revered: the Father honoured; the Son worshipped; the Holy Spirit acknowledged. With a new understanding, a fresh passion and burning urgency, pray: *Our Father, who art in heaven, hallowed be thy name.*

The
Fourth
Commandment

Remember the Sabbath day, to keep it holy
(Exod. 20:8).

The Sabbath was made for man, not man for the Sabbath; the Son of Man is Lord of the Sabbath (Mark 2:27).

'Sabbath' means 'ceasing' and therefore 'resting'. The Sabbath is a loving gift to us, so we can 'cease' from the rush of living, and rest in God. Since our Lord rose on the first day of the week, Christians have celebrated Sunday, the Lord's Day, as a Day of Rest.

Lord, I need a Day of Rest.

I'm even more busy since I became involved in church. As well as work and family, there are now other activities – evenings out, extra meetings, letters to write, people to see. Life has become so hectic. I hardly have time to think.

Lord, I need to appreciate Your Day of Rest.

How good to be with You in worship
the Day You surprised Mary Magdalene in the garden, as dawn came and she lingered alone overcome by sorrow;
the Day You met Simon Peter, after he had denied You three times, and You forgave and restored him;

the Day You joined Cleopas on the dusty road of life, and his heart burned as You shared with him things concerning Yourself;

the Day You breathed Your Spirit on Your trembling disciples as they hid in the upper room;

the Day You confronted Thomas, with all his doubts, and he worshipped You as Lord and God.

Lord, I need to enjoy the gift of Your Day.

Even when my shift work falls on Sunday, I still make time to be with You; when the week has been too full, the ironing needs doing, the garden needs weeding, the car needs washing, I must still preserve the luxury of Your gift of rest; when the fever of life intrudes, and the rush and bustle tries to rob me of Your peace, I must still guard the gift of Your Day.

My Child,
This is the secret of enduring: to be still and know that I am God.
This is the art of renewal: to rest and be quiet before Me.
This is the way of growth in faith: to share in the worship of My Name –
For they who wait on Me will renew their strength,
they shall mount up with wings as eagles,
they shall run and not be weary,
they shall walk and not faint.

The Fourth Commandment
The Sabbath Day

Remember the Sabbath day by keeping it holy.
Six days you shall labour and do all your work,
but the seventh day is a Sabbath to the LORD your
God. On it you shall not do any work....
(Exod. 20:8-10).

The Lord's Day has become a burning issue. We all know the Sunday observance of forty years ago is today being eroded. We all know, too, that this matter has been legislated on by our Parliament in recent years and the signal sent out to the nation that there is little or no need to keep Sunday special. What is not so widely known is that the Social Chapter of the Maastricht Treaty, which our government wants to ignore, lays down that trading should cease each weekend for thirty six hours. It's surely significant that after fifty years of so-called 'continental Sundays', European governments are now wanting to make Sunday trading illegal. On the other hand, our government is refusing to learn from the bitter experience of others and wants to make it legal. How blind can people be?

Before we come to the fourth commandment, may I make two introductory points? The *first* is that we have to deplore a legalistic attitude to the Lord's Day. In the Gospels are well-known stories which illustrate the narrow legalism in Jesus' day (e.g. see Mark 2:1-12; 3:1-6). Sabbath observance had reached absurd proportions. For example, the Jewish Rabbis laid down that if a wall fell on top of someone on the Sabbath, only enough rubble could be removed to find out how badly the person was injured. If he was not injured too badly, then he must be left until the Sabbath ended, when the rescue could be completed. In Israel today, lifts in hotels stop automatically on the Sabbath at every floor to avoid anyone having to push the button, and so 'work' on the Sabbath day!

That kind of zeal for the law is quite against the spirit of the fourth commandment, as the Lord points out when he says: *The Sabbath was made for man, not man for the Sabbath* (Mark 2:27).

The *second* comment is that the Sabbath pattern was far more deeply embedded into Jewish society than many of us realise. As well as a weekly Sabbath, there were yearly Sabbaths. Every Sabbath (i.e. seventh) year, fields had to be left fallow, to rest. So Israel practised a kind of rotation, and a farmer would have each year at least one field that would be resting. That's just one example of the Sabbath year, the seventh year.

But most important of all was the Year of Jubilee, which came after seven Sabbath years. Seven times seven is forty-nine, so the fiftieth year was the year of Jubilee. It was a year of restoration. That year, all property was returned to its original owner. If your uncle had been a bad manager, and sold off the family business or farm, in the Year of Jubilee the new owner must restore it to the family of its original owner. The price paid for it would have taken into consideration the number of years still to run before the next Year of Jubilee. And this was all part of a system built around the passing of seven sabbath years.

In other words, the weekly Sabbath was only the tip of the iceberg because nine-tenths of the Sabbath was below water, hardly seen. But it was there, and social law as well as property law, hung upon the Sabbath concept. We need to bear in mind that the Sabbath was the foundation of far more than a pattern of work, rest and play.

The Sabbath is built into creation as a gift

Nine of the Ten Commandments begin with straight imperatives: *You shall... You shall not....* But the fourth commandment is different. It begins, *Remember...* because it takes us right back to Creation, and to the cycle of the seven day week, with the seventh day as a rest day, as ordained from the beginning of human history.

'Sabbath' literally means 'ceasing'. On the seventh day, God rested. He ceased from all his work. And so we are to understand that God gave us a wonderful gift, a day when we can cease from the busyness of our work, and be at peace. A day when we can be still and quiet. A day when we can recover.

I once knew a man who was a dreadful driver.

He would drive along for miles in third gear, forgetting to change up into fourth gear. Or he would forget to change down, and would be talking away while the car jerked its way up hills at 10 m.p.h. but still in fourth. He ruined any car he drove, because a car is designed to be used in a certain way, and the driver who ignores basic principles is asking for trouble.

God has designed each one of us to live in a certain way. We have not been constructed to force ourselves forward, day after day, without any rest. We are fearfully and wonderfully made. As well as needing sleep, food, warmth and fresh air, as well as needing love, friendship and companionship, we also need rest and quietness.

I understand that a very high proportion of the prescriptions doctors write are for tranquillisers or sedatives. This is because in our modern foolishness, we have produced a frenetic society: people constantly rushing about – if not working, frantically playing or throwing themselves into a hundred and one things, forgetting to 'cease', to stop, to be still.

Many of us actually need to be protected from ourselves. (I know; I am someone who needs to be protected from myself). There are those of us who take on more and more and more. We find it hard to say no. Some take home bulging briefcases from the office with work they are going to do on Sunday. Others are drawn into sports clubs, or social clubs, or flying clubs or whatever, all of which are determined to use the one free day in the week to pursue their activities. Children who once attended a Bible Class on Sundays are taken off by the school into the hills for 'leisure' hikes. And so the 'ceasing', the stopping, is lost. And fewer and fewer people know how to be still and at rest.

I am glad that at least the Trades Unions have tried to protect their members from exploitation. Insisting on 'double time' pay for Sunday work discourages employers from asking their employees to work unnecessarily on Sundays. Workers do need to be guarded from unscrupulous employers who would work them seven days a week to try and increase turnover. The Trades Unions have been in the vanguard of the fight to keep Sunday special. And we must be grateful to them that they are prepared to work to preserve time for families to be together.

Our society, however, with its voracious appetite for more money, or more pleasure, or more football, or more racing, or more activity, would very soon swallow up every free minute of every free hour that anyone has, ignoring our deep psychological, as well as physical, needs to cease, to be still, to stop, one day in seven.

Gifts generally fall into one of two categories: those which are eminently useful, and those which we don't really need or want. It's always rather embarrassing to receive something which one will never find any real use for. But it's good to receive a gift and be able to say enthusiastically, 'That's just what I have been needing!'

I remember a Jumble Sale I was at years ago in a very wealthy district on the south side of a great city. One stall at the sale struck me. It was an 'unused gifts' stall. The items up for sale were birthday or Christmas gifts which no one had wanted. They had been opened, admired, then put away in a drawer. Now, at last, they had been donated to the Jumble Sale to raise money for the Scouts. Beautiful things they were. A new electric razor, going for £1. A set of expensive hair brushes with mahogany handles going for 50p. An 18 piece bone-china tea set for £1.50. A solid silver photograph frame for 30p. I couldn't believe my eyes. Lovely gifts that had been unwanted.

God has given us a gift, a gift we really need – the gift of a day of rest, when we should cease, be still, be at peace. But we are perilously close to selling off God's precious gift for an old song, even though this gift was built into very creation as a gift for our blessing, health and happiness. The Sabbath is God's gift to us.

Society needs a Sabbath

Have you ever noticed the glaring contradictions which come across on television? For example, one programme will be deploring the increase in violent crime and there will be informed discussion on how to combat the violence spreading in our inner city areas. And then the same evening another programme will be a film offering some interesting new ideas on how to steal a car or plan a bank robbery, as the 'baddies' in the film entertain the viewers with violence and robbery. Have you noticed that?

The government knows that family life is breaking down. It is aware of thousands of homeless teenagers sleeping rough. It understands that they have run away from home because of marriage break-ups. It even urges the churches and other charities to try and hold families together in every way they can. Yet it allows the broadcasters constantly to screen programmes which encourage marital infidelity. They license films which make sin appear funny, adultery a joke, and broken homes the norm. All the while, Westminster sheds crocodile tears and laments the breakdown of society. Surely you have noticed the sheer incongruity of all this?

The assault attempted by Baroness Thatcher's government on the Lord's Day completely ignored the significance of Sunday worship in maintaining the closeness of the family. This was in spite of the fact it has been proved that the benefit for families sharing in worship on the Lord's Day is very great. Yet her government posed as the custodian of traditional family values. The successor to that government took the same line and the erosion of the Sabbath rest has continued apace. It appears our nation cannot learn from either history or Scripture.

You see, there is no magic answer to the increasing break-up of family life. The way our society is going, it will become harder and harder to hold families together. Readers who have young children, or who haven't yet any children, will be hard put to hold on to their children when they reach their early teens. If society follows the American pattern, then within another decade or so, we will have millions of teenagers who have left their homes, trudging the roads or living under bridges or on railway stations with no prospect of work or hope for the future.

Is there no defence against such family disaster? Of course there is. Where genuine love fills the home, and children *know* they are really loved, where parents teach their children the Christian faith *at home* – not assuming the job will be done for them by Sunday School or some youth organisation, and where families *worship together*, there is a strong defence against the influences threatening to break up the family in the years to come.

It's an old prescription. Granny and Grandad used it. But it works well, better than any other, if it's used in the right way. The family all together in God's House on the Lord's Day, followed by a family afternoon, with parents taking time to be with the children, giving of themselves, their time and their love. Such a family is preserving like fine gold one day in seven as a day of rest and quiet together. In that way Sunday becomes the highlight of the week, the gracious adhesive that binds the family together. It is wise and necessary for parents to work hard at making the Lord's Day a very special day, with little treats reserved for Sunday and the highest quality of time and affection shared among the family.

Down the past thirty years of my ministry, with both sorrow and joy, I have seen and watched families. On the one hand, I have seen families break up before my eyes – and it could all have been predicted without very much skill, for there was no togetherness from the start. The family were rarely together, and seldom in church, though claiming church membership.

I have also seen families holding rock solid and, with the passing of the years, becoming even closer and more loving. Through school, or college, or into work, the children were growing up and marrying, and starting their own families, but sticking together. The foundation of that closeness and love has been the Lord's Day with all that keeping the Lord's Day together meant.

The interesting thing is this: when there are families which keep God's Day for worship and rest, they are unconsciously doing something else. They are helping to keep a church warm and alive as a place of refuge and comfort to which other families, out in the cold, can come to rebuild and restore their lives too. Just keeping this fourth commandment becomes in itself an act of Christian service – the Sabbath built into society as a need!

Sabbath rest a grace of salvation

The question is sometimes asked: 'Why was the Sabbath the seventh day of the week in the Old Testament, but in the New Testament it is the first day of the week?' The answer is that the Lord's Day is the day when Christ was raised from the dead. It is the day when he appeared to Simon and Mary in the Garden, to Cleopas and his friend on the road to Emmaus, and to the disciples in the upper room. It is the day when the Holy Spirit was poured out at Pentecost. It is the day when the early church came together to break bread.

That is why the day of rest moved from the Jewish Saturday to the Christian Sunday. It was new wineskins for new wine. On the Lord's Day, we remember the glorious work of Christ. That's why we call it *his* Day – 'The Lord's Day'.

The Old Testament Jewish Sabbath was a celebration of *creation*; but the New Testament Lord's Day is a celebration of *redemption*. Great power was used by God in creating this world with its teeming life and fruitful herbage, to say nothing of the wonder of human life. But a *greater power* was used by God in bringing from spiritual death those who are now alive in Christ. In creation, God gave man and woman to each other, but in redemption, God gave us *himself*. In creation, God gave life to Adam, but in redemption, he gave us life in Christ. In creation, we learn of an earthly paradise, but in redemption, we learn of a heavenly paradise. The old is swallowed up into the new.

For you and me, remembering the Lord's Day is part of our new life in Christ. It is part of being a Christian. Our coming together on the first day of the week is in honour of Christ. It's not just that we come together to say, 'Nearly 2000 years ago, the stone was rolled away and Christ was raised from the dead.' Yes, we do say that, but we are saying more. We come expecting to meet with the risen Lord the way Cleopas, Peter, Mary and the others met with him. For his part, he is waiting for us the way he waited for the disciples on the shore after they had fished all night – that event too happened on a Sunday morning. We wait, Sunday by Sunday, for Jesus Christ to visit us, to come to us, to be with us, and show his face and his glory to us; to share with us the blessings of redemption. That is the heart of the Lord's Day and our coming together.

Waiting upon God in Christ is the heart of the Lord's Day because, essentially, worship is meeting with Christ. It is only Christ who can come to each one of us and minister to our needs. Consider the ridiculous impossibility of my preaching a sermon which will be a help to everyone in a congregation, coming as the worshippers inevitably would from such different homes, all with very different problems. The chances would be remote of any preacher hitting on something that might effectively help even half a dozen people. But if Christ meets with that congregation, if they hear his voice, if he searches their hearts and brings them his message, then they will worship him and learn from his word.

On the Lord's Day, therefore, Christ's coming among us must be our expectation. We must come together knowing that waiting for us will be One who will pass along the pews, and stop before each one of us, looking into our minds, seeing our needs, hearing the silent cry of our hearts. And, taking our hand in his, he will point the way forward, which is the way he too is travelling, inviting us to go with him.

He lifts the burdens. He carries the griefs. He forgives the failures. He knows the secrets. And He shares the joys. And being in closest fellowship with Christ and receiving his mercy and love is called entering into the Sabbath rest which God has promised. That is why the Sabbath is built into our salvation as a Grace.

Has Christ come and spoken quietly to your heart as you have been reading today? Then obey Him. His blessing makes rich and adds no sorrow with it.

The
Fifth
Commandment

Honour your father and mother (Exod. 20:12).

Children, obey your parents in the Lord ... Fathers, do not provoke your children... (Eph. 6:1, 4).

The Scriptures teach the responsibility of children towards their parents – to respect and obey them; also, the responsibilities of parents towards their children – to provide a loving and secure environment for them. The fifth commandment reflects right attitudes not only within the family, but also within the Christian congregation and wider community.

Heavenly Father, You have set us in families so that love may be shared and security provided. We thank You for our loved ones:

for mother, and all her work in caring for us,
for father, and his role as head of our family,
for aunts, and their loving interest that has followed us from early days,
for grandparents, and the store of experience they have gathered over the years.

Yet, Father, not always do we appreciate the privilege of our loved ones. There are times when we do not want to listen to their counsel. Often we are convinced we know better, and are determined to go our own way. Sometimes we are irritated that they seem so slow and old-fashioned, and find it hard to think in modern ways.

Make us patient and respectful, Lord, as You were towards Your parents. Willing to consider and listen to their opinions. For a humble spirit, rather than a haughty spirit, leads to wise decisions. Help us to remember they love us, and desire only the best for us.

Lord Jesus, in Your darkest hour of suffering, You were concerned for Your mother, and provided for her. May we, even when we are busiest, think of our loved ones, and make time to visit them, or write to them, or telephone, to show our affection for those who have cared for us all our lives.

We thank You, Lord, that Your Church is a family, and that within its fellowship we have fathers, mothers, brothers, sisters. May we love, honour and respect one another, so that we fulfil Your law of love and bring glory to Your Name.

My child, whoever does the will of God is my brother and sister and mother (Mark 3:35).

The Fifth Commandment
Honouring our Parents

Honour your father and your mother, so that you may live long in the land the Lord your God is giving you (Exod. 20:12).

In the church where I was brought up, and where we worshipped each Sunday as a family, the Ten Commandments were painted in Old English script at the front of the church on the wall behind the communion table. As a boy, when I found the minister's sermon difficult to understand, I used to occupy my mind reading the commandments. Nor do I think that was, for me as a child, a misuse of sermon time!

A feature of this Victorian work of art (as the lettering undoubtedly was) were the titles given to the two columns of writing which made up the Ten Commandments. Above the first panel was the legend, *The First Table;* inscribed below were commandments one to four. Above the second panel was the legend, *The Second Table;* and below were commandments five to ten.

As I read and re-read the commandments of God each Sunday, it was imprinted on my youthful mind that the first four commandments summed up our duty towards God; they made up *The First Table.* The remaining six commandments summed up our duty towards others, and made up *The Second Table*. It was a good lesson for a boy to have learned. (I also learned that the greatest commandment encapsulated *The First Table,* and the second greatest commandment encapsulated *The Second Table*. Mark 12:28ff).

We come now to the fifth commandment, but the first in *The Second Table* – the beginning of our duty towards others. Are we surprised that our first duty to others should be not towards the starving, the destitute or the disadvantaged, but towards our parents?

Respect

I remember being invited to a social evening by a member of one of my former congregations. At least a dozen guests were gathered when my wife and I arrived. To our consternation, our hostess was entertaining her guests by mocking and mimicking her own mother (who was not present). She was calling her names and poking fun at her in a way that was supposed to be amusing. Certainly the assembled company were finding the performance highly entertaining.

I was unable to join in the hilarity that greeted this 'party piece' from our hostess. Indeed, it seemed to me quite shocking – even cruel and evil – that a daughter could show such disrespect towards the one who had brought her into the world, and tended and cared for her in her infancy and through the turbulent years of childhood and adolescence. I felt what was happening was grieving to God, for it was a direct violation of the fifth commandment.

A young couple once came to me to arrange their wedding. As they sat in my study, the prospective groom began criticising his mother. He waxed more and more eloquent, calling her dreadful names and maligning her quite viciously. I looked at his fiancée, and it was in my heart to say to her, 'Lassie, beware of a man who can speak like that of his mother! You are being given a preview of how he may well treat *you* in ten years' time.' Honouring our parents most certainly begins with respecting them.

Bad parents

Someone may respond and ask, 'But just say my parent is a contemptible person, what then?' The answer is easy. We are not asked to close our eyes to the failings or wrong-doings of our parents. Nevertheless, because they are our parents, we are to show them respect at all times. King Saul was a parent who opened his life to the powers of evil until those powers possessed him. In his wicked fury, he threw a javelin at his own son Jonathan. Though Jonathan was grieved and angry, he never once showed disrespect for his father. Read the story again to see how nobly Jonathan behaved in the most difficult family circumstances (1 Sam. 14, 19, 20).

Obedience

'Honour', however, means more than 'respect'. It also means 'obedience'. This is increasingly a thorny problem today. So many parents tell me that their children, especially teenage children, no longer take any notice of what they say. When it comes to the time they should be in at night, how they spend their free time and many other basic domestic and family matters, parents' wishes can be disregarded entirely, so it seems.

Young people who may be reading this book, the commandment of God is that you obey your parents. Teenagers should read in Luke 2:51 how the Lord Jesus was *obedient to his parents*. Moreover, that obedience appears to have been his response as a son until he was thirty years of age.

Someone might object, 'But just say my parents order me to do something I believe to be wrong?' I think of a girl I know well who came from an unbelieving family, and who was forbidden to attend church when she became a Christian. What was she to do? The New Testament qualifies our obedience: it has to be *in the Lord* (Eph. 6:1). Take Jonathan again as an example. Saul demanded his son help him to kill David (1 Sam. 20:31ff), but Jonathan rightly refused. He even helped David to escape Saul's assassination attempt.

I would suggest, however, that very rarely in the West today would any parent's orders go against the laws of God. The fifth commandment stands, therefore, with this plain meaning that honouring our parents must include obeying them *in the Lord, for this is right* (Eph. 6:1).

Good parents
There is, of course, another side to parenting! Paul makes a balanced statement when he follows up the command that children should *obey their parents in the Lord* with his exhortation, *Fathers, do not exasperate your children...* (Eph. 6:4). Those of us who are parents must not discourage our children or be overbearing or intolerant with them. Our children must never feel that they have been rejected, nor that they have forfeited our affection through their wrong-doing.

The model for every Christian parent is the Heavenly Parent whose lovingkindness and faithful care is never compromised by his standards of holiness and truth. God loves us without ever indulging us, on the one hand; and he disciplines us without casting us off, on the other hand. His word is completely reliable: he always says what he means and means what he says. We know we can depend on him utterly.

So let us encourage our children to observe this fifth commandment by ourselves being always gracious though firm, always loving though never soft, always considerate without over-indulgence. Let us love our children as our Father has loved us. Let us make it a pleasure for them to obey the fifth commandment.

Old age

It is always a pleasure when one is visiting an elderly person to hear her saying with pride, 'My son gave me that … my son calls every evening to see me … my son will attend to that for me.' So it should be. For honouring our parents also means caring for them in their old age.

Once during a pastoral visit I listened to as sad a tale as I have heard for many years. The elderly widow said (her story was later confirmed by relatives and neighbours), that though her son lived only a stone's throw away he never came near her from one year's end to another, unless it was to ask for money. The Lord Jesus had a most stern rebuke for religious people of his day who failed to provide for their parents in their old age (Mark 7:9ff). The fact that Jesus had to name this sin tells us that it is as old as humankind. It is not just a problem of our modern selfishness. This form of dishonouring parents has always been a sin busy people must guard against.

I know that in our welfare state, there is no need for any elderly parent to be unprovided for. But we all know that quality of life can have little to do with mere material provision. The elderly must be cherished, listened to, and respected, most especially by their own sons and daughters. They should be gladly given the status that is rightly theirs and treated for what they are – 'elders'.

I am glad that I am able to comment that, for the most part, believing sons and daughters I have known have carried the finest of Christian testimonies in their communities in this regard. Graciously, lovingly and in the most godly way, they have honoured their parents throughout their old age, and so have fulfilled the Royal Law of Love.

Understanding the commandments

In the past, there have been some very fanciful interpretations of Old Testament passages. We have all heard sermons where stories are spiritualised, and meanings taken from them, or else imposed upon them, which simply do not have the ring of authenticity. We have been left wondering whether this is really what God is saying to us from this text. Let me give an example. When Thomas à Becket was murdered in the cathedral by some knights of Henry II, the Archbishop of York preached a sermon on the state of the Church in England, and took as his text the cry of the fevered son of the Shunammite woman, 'My head, my head!' (2 Kings 4:19). The burden of his sermon was to say that the Church was in a fevered and sick state. I think most of us would recognise that the Archbishop's interpretation of the passage was highly suspect – and that's an understatement if ever there was one!

When we come to any Old Testament text or passage, we must look for certain things. First, for the original meaning – what did these words mean to those who heard them when they were first spoken? Second, we must also look for the timeless principles which apply to the people of God of all generations. Third, we look too for any pointers forward to Christ. Let's apply these three criteria to this fifth commandment.

Our social circle
In Old Testament times, it went without saying that older men and women were given special respect. Today in many eastern cultures, older people are afforded immense respect on account of their age. When I visited Korea some years ago, I was immensely impressed by the way in which older people were given a dignity and status in both family and society simply because of their years.

Notice that the principle of respect towards our parents must be extended beyond the immediate family circle into the wider social circle in which we happen to live. In other words, the commandment, as it was originally given and intended, is teaching us to honour and respect all those older than ourselves.

Western society today has taken something of a sharp turn off in another direction at this point. We tend to give more prominence to youth. Old age has become dreaded, even despised. Some adults (of both sexes) spend a great deal of time and money trying to conceal the evidence of their age, and they present themselves as far younger than they really are. Creams are applied to the skin, dye to the hair, and elixirs are distilled from the most unlikely sources (including the sex glands of tomcats), all in the desperate attempt to hold back the relentless march of time and approach of old age.

The story is told of an elderly man entering a packed theatre in ancient Athens. Not one Athenian rose to offer him a seat. Then the ambassador from Sparta rose and gave the old man his seat, saying, 'Athens knows what is right, but will not do it.'

Young people of our generation need to learn their manners from the Word of God. The Scriptures say, *Rise in the presence of the aged, show respect for the elderly, and revere your God* (Lev. 19:32). Parents should teach both their children and teenagers to stand up when older people enter a room. Such manners ennoble; they do not demean.

The church elders

I am sure most practising Christians would all agree that an important body such as the elders of the church need a good balance of youth and age. We need the progressive, creative thinkers who are in touch with what is happening in society. But alongside that, we also need to temper inexperience by experience; youth needs to be counter-balanced by the wisdom of the years.

The younger elders with their zeal and imagination are like the great canvas sheet of the sail that catches the wind, driving the sailing boat forward through the water. In contrast, the elderly with their maturity and understanding are like the heavy keel beneath the boat, without which it would keel over and capsize. With both sail and keel, the bows of the boat cut through waves in safety.

Mind you, there is nothing quite as deadening and stultifying as a controlling group of church elders composed entirely of aged men with no visions or dreams – all keel and no wide canvas to catch the breath of the Spirit. However, where there are younger elders, let them learn to honour and respect the older elders. Likewise, let not the older elders despise the younger elders because of their comparative youth.

Of course the biblical word 'elder' does not have a primary reference to age as such. Elders were chosen more for their wisdom, maturity and experience. One possible derivation of the word 'elder' is 'bearded one' and when we remember that relatively young men are quite capable of growing beards, we will realise that it is the quality of the potential elder's experience of God and his work which should direct the church's consideration and appointment.

Those who have been given the status of elder, should be honoured, respected and even obeyed by the church members. This is unquestionably a fulfilment of one aspect of the fifth commandment. For their part, elders should recognise that they too have great responsibilities towards those over whom they have been set as overseers: they must care for them as an under-shepherd, taking Christ the Chief Shepherd as their example of service and love.

Our employers

We must remember that when the fifth commandment was originally given, the father was almost invariably the employer. Only occasionally do fathers employ their sons and daughters today. Nevertheless, the principle enshrined here lives on. It is that Christians must show respect and honour towards their employers. Whether we work in the public or private sectors, if we reverence God, we will also reverence those over us at work.

It was when the people of God were at a disastrously low ebb spiritually that *every man did that which was right in his own eyes* (Judg. 21:25). In modern society, there is an attitude of licence and irresponsibility abroad which savagely violates the spirit of this fifth commandment. Indeed, in many communities there are factories, staffrooms and offices where any who seek seriously to show honour and respect to their bosses are ostracized.

Christians need to be alert to the movement to secularise those more conservative communities where older values still hold good. In many cities and industrial areas, these values have been dismissed as outmoded and replaced with a cavalier attitude towards authority which has within it the seeds of a lawlessness approaching anarchy. There is urgent need for Christians to act as salt and light in society. God-fearing employees can stem the tide by carrying the principle of the fifth commandment into their everyday living and working. Respect for authority by Christians at work on the one hand, balanced by the kind of employers who by their high principles and fair treatment of their employees earn and deserve respect on the other hand, will have a leavening effect on society.

The promise
Notice the fifth commandment is the first with a promise. I used to think the promise of the fifth commandment referred solely to longevity: *...that you may live long in the land*.... However, such an understanding limits the meaning of the promise, which properly refers to the security of tenure of God's people in the land, though there is no need to exclude entirely from the promise the suggestion of long life.

In our New Testament era, the people of God are now scattered throughout the whole world. We live, not in that tiny strip of land along the eastern shore of the Mediterranean Sea, but in every place where God has set us. So the promise is to each fellowship of God's people. We shall survive – more, prosper and grow in the coming years – as we incorporate into our attitudes the great principle of honour and respect for our elders. God is promising here to bless the communities where the fifth commandment is taken seriously.

We have all been in homes where the children have been badly behaved, ill-mannered and disobedient, so much so that we have been relieved to get away. We have also been in homes where the atmosphere of love and harmony arising from real respect was a pleasure to witness. How much more secure and happy is the latter kind of home!

What kind of 'family' is our home congregation? Would a stranger be impressed at once by the mutual respect, care and honour we show one another? The presence of God in your fellowship will only be strong when the members are loyal, faithful, respectful and caring towards each other.

Mutual respect which is built on humility towards, and reverence for, others is the God-ordained means of achieving harmony in any congregation. Conversely, it is pride and indifference towards the rights of others which causes disruption and quarrelling in a church. This is why Paul wrote, *Love must be sincere ... Be devoted to one another in brotherly love. Honour one another above yourselves ... Live in harmony with one another. Do not be proud, but be willing to associate with people of low position. Do not be conceited* (Rom. 12:9ff).

Surely we would all acknowledge our Lord faithfully lived out such an attitude in his daily life while here on earth. *Who, being in very nature God, did not consider equality with God something to be grasped, but made himself nothing, taking the very nature of a servant ... Your attitude should be the same as that of Christ Jesus* (Phil. 2:6ff). He above all others fulfilled this fifth commandment in all that he did and was among us. It is his will that we follow his example.

The
Sixth
Commandment

You shall not kill (Exod. 20:13).

Anyone who hates his brother is a murderer (1 John 3:15).

But I say to you, 'Love your enemies and pray for those who persecute you, so that you may be sons of your Father in heaven' (Matt. 5:44-45).

In the Sermon on the Mount, our Lord expounds the sixth commandment as forbidding the emotion of unrighteous anger. He then applies this principle to losing one's temper, to cruel gossip, and to the sneering insult (Matt. 5:21-22).

Lord, when I read the sixth commandment, I congratulated myself that here at last was a law I had never broken. I was proud, and ready to give myself credit as an upright citizen. I went on to think harshly of those who have taken the life of another.

Until, Lord, I stumbled on Your words about this Law. And I found You saw the seeds of murder in unjust anger, in gossip and in sneers. And then the sword of Your mouth wounded me, and the light of Your eye opened my heart to me, and I discovered the broken fragments of this terrible commandment littering my life.

I remember, Lord, my intense irritation whenever that person appears. How he annoys me! It's a clash of personalities, and he can't help it; but I feel such anger welling up in me. There have even been times when I have hated him, Lord.

I remembered a conversation about a colleague. We stirred up a teaspoonful of fiction with a tablespoonful of hearsay and a pinch of *possible fact*, and the mixture we made was cruel and insulting. We murdered a reputation that day.

I remembered my biting sarcasm, the cutting wit of my words, which made some laugh, but my victim winced in pain as my arrows found their target.

Lord, my complacency shrivels up when Your word falls on me. I find that I am guilty, even before this Law.

My child, if the commandment wounds you, it is only so that I may heal you. And I heal that you may learn to love, as I have loved you. Together, you and I, we must pray for those who grieve and hurt us. We must win them by our love. My love in you. For the greatest power on earth is love.

The Sixth Commandment
No Murder!

You shall not murder (Exod. 20:13).

The Apostle Paul tell us that *the law is spiritual* (Rom. 7:14). Paul didn't dream that up himself. It was God who laid down that obedience to the sixth commandment was far more than refraining from murder, for we read in Leviticus, *You shall not **hate** your brother in your heart* (19:17).

When preachers are expounding the ten commandments, and they reach the sixth, they almost invariably hurry over the question of murder and direct most of their sermon negatively to the subject of hatred, and positively to the subject of love. They tend to go to that part of the Sermon on the Mount (Matt. 5:21ff), where our Lord shows us that we can violate the sixth commandment in our hearts, and do violence to a person through hatred, slander or gossip. After all, we all know that many a reputation and good name have been 'murdered' without ever a blow being struck. That form of sin becomes the main burden of the exposition. Of course that is quite correct.

However it is surely necessary to consider the actual subject of murder as well as the manifestations of bitterness and hatred which too often lurk in the human heart. It is not just that the murder rate in Northern Ireland has been so phenomenally high during the tragic decades of the political troubles there. We tend to forget that in the United Kingdom and right across Europe crimes of violence and murder have been dramatically increasing since the 1960s. In 1991, there were 92 fatal stabbings in the city of Glasgow alone!

Revenge

The sixth commandment has only two words in the original Hebrew: *No murder*. But it is important to note that the word used generally describes *violent action taken in revenge*.

There is great confusion in our generation over this word 'revenge'. Our Bibles draw a clear distinction between revenge killing by an individual on the one hand, and execution by the state on the other hand. The two are not synonymous in Biblical thinking. We are all aware of many voices today urging that violent murder on the one hand and the death penalty legally administered on the other hand are exactly the same. At this point in our argument, it is sufficient simply to deny categorically that they are the same, and to assert that in biblical thought revenge is unilateral action by one person (or family, as in a feud), meting out a personal, private sentence.

Taking the commandment to include the prohibition of violent action by one person against another, we can immediately see three contemporary applications.

Personal revenge

Let us take two examples from events in the United Kingdom within our own lifetime. One man's teenage daughter was savagely stabbed to death on Wimbledon Common, while a young couple's two-year-old son was abducted by two eleven-year-old boys, brutally killed and then callously mutilated. We all feel deeply for those parents who have suffered so greatly through these wicked murders, and we can understand when their grief is mingled with fierce anger against those who have violently robbed them of their children and the precious gift of life. When we hear their cries for justice and their threats against the convicted murderers, we hesitate to condemn the emotions fermenting in their hearts. What parent cannot empathise with the intensity of such feelings?

But that is exactly the sense in which the commandment says, *No murder.* It means that those broken-hearted parents may not take their own revenge against the guilty, should they discover who they are. The sixth commandment means, *No murder for personal revenge.*

Racism

But the command goes further with a second contemporary application. It also means, *No racial hatred.* Most of us have forgotten how many Russians died in the Second World War. The figure is an astounding twenty million. We have forgotten how many Jews went to the gas chambers: it was

100

six million. And all that slaughter arose from racial hatred. It's hard to take it in, is it not?

Racial hatred was alive and active in Christ's day. It is alive and active in our day too. It sets the Basque against the Spaniard; the Breton against the Frenchman; the Quebecois against the Canadian; the Croat against the Serb; the Serb against the Bosnian; the Irish against the Ulsterman; the Ulsterman against the native Irish; the Scots, Welsh and Irish against the English; many English against the Pakistani and West Indian.

In both England and Scotland, there have been recent developments of racism which are causes of great concern. Even when a government tries to legislate against this evil, it seeps out under the doors which Acts of Parliament seek in vain to shut fast to keep it locked away.

Racism can start so innocently. It appeals to our sense of loyalty, to our traditions and all we hold dear. It appeals to us to safeguard our proud history, our flag and all the other symbols of national identity which appear to be threatened. Nevertheless, racial hatred is easily the world leader in causing this sixth commandment to be violated. More deaths in our world have been inspired by racial hatred than any other single cause.

There are evidences in most communities of the fruits of racial hatred. Those who live in Northern Ireland have only to travel beyond Newry to the border with the Republic to witness the massive security arrangements which have been made necessary by racial hatred. The seemingly innocent and tiny village of Middletown on the border of Monaghan has been turned into a grim fortress by the excesses of racism and its bitter consequences. Yet the commandment clearly states, *No murder – no revenge killing.*

Political violence
The third contemporary application of the commandment must be, *No violence for political ends.* It's not often that the respectable, middle-class Ulster Unionist betrays his deepest feelings about 'The Troubles' (as the political turmoil of thirty years has been called). He leaves such vulgarity to the so-called sectarian bigots. However I recall several earnest conversations with men who were highly respected in both church and community who confided in me that they wished the Protestant paramilitaries would send a bullet between the eyes of some of Sinn Fein's leaders. 'That would be', they confided, 'a positive step towards sorting out our problems.'

Yet here we have the entrance to the three steps which lead down into the spiral of political violence. Step one is always the failure to forgive – at least, genuinely to offer forgiveness. Step two is the feud, for when you and I harbour a grudge, unable and unwilling to forgive, we are drawn into a feud. And step three is some kind of action to claim payment for what we see as debts owed to us from the feud. It is that third step which leads into the abyss of violence.

Think of the assassination attempt on Hitler in which Rommel and the theologian Bonhoeffer were implicated. As a result, Rommel, fine general and man of integrity that he was, had to take the poison given him by the Gestapo as the only alternative to court martial, public humiliation and execution. Bonhoeffer was imprisoned and ultimately executed. But would the assassination of Hitler have solved the problem of Nazism? Undoubtedly, had Hitler been killed in that attempt on his life, he would immediately have been succeeded by men of the same breed. Nazism needed to be defeated *per se*.

History confirms that the use of violence for political ends is futile. The harsh despotic rule of the Bourbon kings in France gave way to an even harsher, more despotic rule by Bonaparte, and so the flower of French manhood perished on the battlefields of the Napoleonic Wars. The rule of the Czars gave way in 1917 to the even more despotic rule of Marxism. The Kaiser gave way to Hitler. Even Cromwell could not retain the power he won by force, without the continued, ruthless use of that same force. Were the leaders of the IRA to be shot by paramilitaries, equally violent men would step into their shoes – there can be no doubt about that.

The sixth commandment, then, condemns also the use of violence for political ends: *No murder!*

Words spoken by the mouth of God, and written by his very finger. Would to God that this commandment was faithfully taught in the pulpits and classrooms of our land today.

Action by the State

A difficult question arises. Is the Bible teaching pacifism, and even when a murderous dictator such as Hitler seizes power, is there no resistance at all that may be offered? In other words, is it God's will that we refuse to resist and allow the evil tyrant to pursue every kind of wickedness unhindered?

When I was still at school in the 1950s and two years of 'National Service' in the armed forces was the prospect for every sixth-form boy, the subject of *pacifism* was hotly debated by most seventeen and eighteen-year-olds. It was debated because the option was there for a young man to appeal against those two years of enforced service in the armed forces by pleading he was a *conscientious objector,* meaning that in all conscience he could have nothing to do in any way with an organisation that was licensed to kill, as the forces are in times of war. But pacifism is hard to justify on the basis of the sixth commandment. (By pacifism I mean the view that violence must always and without exception be met with non-violence).

The words, *No murder,* as I have tried to show already in this chapter, mean, *No violent (revenge) killing.* We have seen that revenge is to be understood as personal, unilateral action. What Scripture teaches is that we are not to take the law into our own hands. *Vengeance is mine; I will repay, says the Lord* (Rom. 12:19). Someone immediately asks, 'How does God repay?' The answer is by using the State to mete out just retribution. That is why in Romans 13 Paul immediately goes on to deal with the role of the State in this matter.

The defence of the realm
The principle laid down in Romans 13 is that it is the duty of the State to defend its citizens against violence, whether from within by criminal elements, or from without by some foreign power trying to take over by military force. Paul says that the State is *God's servant, an agent of wrath to bring punishment on the wrong doer* (v. 4b). The context makes clear that he is writing about the State resisting violence by using what today many would call 'violence'.

The difference between the State acting and the individual acting must be that while the individual will be motivated by the passion for revenge, the State will be motivated by the desire for justice. The two are not the same. The motivation for revenge is emotional, accompanied by deep passions. The motivation for justice should be calm, unemotional, objective and manifestly fair. That is not to suggest that the father whose daughter was stabbed to death and the parents whose two-year-old was wickedly killed are not also motivated by the desire for justice. It is however to recognise that the individual's desire for justice to be meted out may well also be mingled with feelings of revenge, and that such feelings may not be trusted to be objective and impartial.

So whenever and wherever there is violence against its citizens, the State, according to biblical teaching, should protect them. We should not have to protect ourselves. Whenever citizens do have to protect themselves because the State is not doing it, then society – or at least sections of it – is breaking down, anarchy is creeping in, and law and order are also beginning to break down.

This is the sense in which we must understand the sixth commandment, *No murder! No revenge killing!* – because the State is there fulfilling its responsibility towards peace-loving citizens and protecting them. Paul argues in Romans 13 that this is why we pay our taxes. The State must have the resources to fulfil this as its prime duty to guard us from men and women of violence. The sixth commandment is assuming the defence of the realm to be in place and the State is performing its God-ordained duty.

A harvest of violence

We are all aware that capital punishment was abolished by Act of Parliament some forty years ago. What we tend to forget is that the pressure came from humanists. We can understand the view of the humanist. He does not believe in life after death, therefore he feels compelled to argue that the life of the most twisted, perverted killer should be preserved. Not wanting to appear intellectually unrespectable, many leading churchmen have supported the humanist view.

With each passing year, however, more pressing and obvious becomes the evidence that murder and violence increase in direct proportion to the lighter sentences meted out on the criminal by the courts. In other words, the more kindly and humane the sentences imposed on the violent offender, the more violence and murder there is.

When I was a boy in the 1940s and 50s, there were about five or six murders each year in Scotland. There are now hundreds of murders each year here, though such killings do not catch the headlines in the way sectarian killings in Northern Ireland have tended to do. But nearly one hundred stabbings outside public houses in one year in Glasgow alone make violent murders so common that they are no longer news. Only the most horrendous killings catch the headlines. Murder has now become as common in the towns and cities of our land as burglary was forty years ago. Yet before capital punishment was abolished, only five or six murders in Scotland occurred in any year.

I want to question very seriously the views of the powerful humanist lobby which has been followed by our Parliament. Is it not morally wrong, invariably preserving the lives of self-confessed, violent murderers. The great majority of the population certainly would think so.

The need for capital punishment

We read in Genesis 9 of the covenant God made with Noah after the Flood. God was to protect the world from massive natural disasters which could destroy life on this planet. And part of the covenant with Noah had this provision: *Whoever sheds the blood of man, by man shall his blood be shed; for in the image of God has God made man.*

As far as I myself can determine, that covenant condition has never been revoked in the New Testament. For some years, I wondered whether the death of Christ had some cosmic efficacy under what theologians call 'general grace' – that is, divine grace offered to all humanity irrespective of faith in Christ – which might justify the abolition of this principle. But after years of reflection, it seems to me that Romans 13 confirms that the provision of Genesis 9 still holds firm.

Sincere and godly churchmen have used many arguments against capital punishment. But their arguments have either been emotionally or politically based. They argue, for example, that no one has the right to deprive another of his life, or that many a murderer has come to faith in Christ and become a changed man. Or they argue that if the death penalty was to be restored, our nation would be classed along with governments which are tyrannies.

Of course, the churchmen who have fallen in with the humanists' view of the State urge that they want to see a more compassionate society. I am sure we all want that – only an anarchist would not want it! But all we have seen as a result of so-called compassionate laws has been a steady, relentless and truly terrifying increase in violence of every kind. Instead of our country becoming more compassionate, it has become more dangerous, more bloody, more cruel, more violent.

The Christian Scriptures' answer is: *Whoever sheds the blood of man, by man shall his blood be shed.*

Here is a quotation from a recent issue of a weekly newspaper which serves a respectable, middle-class locality: 'Sex, violence and death, that's the package on offer at our town's cinema these days, and our hundreds of avid cinema fans can't get enough of it.' The truth is that many feed their minds on the very violence we claim to deplore.

A caring people
What is to be our practical, daily response to the sixth commandment? We are to be a caring people! We are to be deeply concerned about violence on the screens. We are therefore to refuse to be entertained by violence, which arguably is one of the main influences that motivates the murderers who stalk our streets. We are to care by being courteous road users, driving with consideration for others, because the motor car in irresponsible hands can be a violent killer. If we are employers we are to care by taking thought for the safety,

health and wellbeing of our employees. We are to care by showing the love of Christ in every way we can, every day of our lives.

Yes, there are those who urge that some murderers have been changed and have even made their peace with God which would have been impossible had capital punishment been administered. To such an argument we must answer that because we believe in life after death, we are to care that more people are not murdered before they have the chance to make their peace with God. The sixth commandment's concern is primarily for the majority rather than for those who have robbed innocent people of the precious gift of life. In perfect harmony with the divine law which led to our Lord's substitutionary death on Calvary, this commandment is motivated by the principle that the soul who sins shall die. It is through the atoning death of Christ that every kind of sinner, including murderers, may find forgiveness, peace with God and hope for a bright future in the life which awaits beyond death.

The
Seventh
Commandment

You shall not commit adultery (Exod. 20:14).

For this reason a man shall leave his father and mother and be united to his wife, and the two shall become one (Matt. 19:5).

The seventh commandment is expounded for us by our Lord (Matt. 5:27f) who would have us understand it not just in terms of the outward act of obedience but also in terms of the inward thought and motive. Paul speaks of bringing every thought captive into the obedience of Christ.

Father God, You have given the privilege of marriage to many, though not to all. As Your loving gift, the union of mind and soul and body is exquisitely beautiful.

We thank You, Lord, for the romantic love of that young man and woman:
    for their delight in each other,
    for their excitement as they prepare for their wedding day;
we thank You for the loving devotion of so many happily married couples:
    for his tender love for her,
    for her fulfilment in loving him utterly in return;

we thank You for that elderly pair who have just celebrated their golden wedding:

for the memory of fifty years together,

for all the loving help given in times of need; help us to rejoice, as You do, Lord, with those who rejoice!

Lord God, hear our prayers for some whose marriages have lost the sparkle and joy of love. You only know the cause –

if it has been selfishness

so that love has been withheld,

if it has been a false reliance on material things

so that love has been misdirected,

if it has been the turning of affections to another

so that love has been stolen;

by Your own great love, turn such hearts back to Yourself, that in loving You, they may love each other, and so rediscover the grace of life.

We remember one who has been left alone, whose life is bruised and broken by the pain of separation. Only those who have experienced such rejection can understand the anguish endured each day. Lord Jesus, You were rejected, and You can come near and enfold in Your arms the desolate life, binding up the wounds, and healing the broken heart.

Hear our prayer, and let our cry come to You.

The Seventh Commandment
Marriage

You shall not commit adultery (Exod. 20:14).

When we compare the moral standards of two generations ago and the standards which hold in society today, it is quite clear that a massive change has taken place. If she were still alive today, what would granny's reaction be to the videos on hire in every High Street? or to the magazines on sale in the newsagents? or to the films shown both before and after 9 pm on television? or to the books stocked by your local bookseller? What has happened? What has gone wrong? Why this enormous change in public standards of morality?

Moral decline
There are various factors which have combined to bring society to the state of moral decline in which we find ourselves today. We have space only to touch on two of these. First, there is contraception. The age-long deterrent of the unwanted child is now redundant, because various methods of birth control have made possible so-called 'safe-sex'. (I say 'so-called' because it is now becoming apparent that women who are promiscuous from their teen years are increasingly liable to develop cervical cancer. This serious condition has developed among younger women in tandem with

greater sexual freedom.) In the past it was generally recognised that children needed a secure, stable environment, and so women refused casual liaisons because of the obvious danger of pregnancy. No longer is that the case.

The ironical aspect of 'safe-sex' is that along with the fall in moral standards has come a dramatic rise in marriage breakdowns. Consequently we have the very problem we thought we could avoid – unwanted children! There are more children in care today in the United Kingdom than ever before in our history. Further, there are more unwanted teenage pregnancies than anywhere else in Europe!

Second, there is the shift away from a generally accepted emphasis on keeping lifelong *promises* to a new obsession with the exaltation of the *emotions*. What do I mean? Simply this, that the marriage promises were once kept out of a determined sense of *duty*. Once a man and woman had made vows, then as a first priority of living they stood by those vows. Now however the first priority is *self-fulfilment*, and with the 'ego' as the 'sun' around which our little 'universe' orbits, how a person *feels* has become the dominant factor in determining the duration of a relationship. 'Love' has become like measles – you contract the disease, but then you recover from it.

Bring these two together – modern contraceptive devices and the obsession with self-fulfilment, then fuel that obsession with images and stories thrown at us by the media, stir it all up with the propaganda that 'everyone is doing it', and we have the prescription for wholesale moral decline. Far more could be said, but space forbids.

An astonishing contrast

It has to be admitted that this seventh commandment is the most surprising of all the commandments. You see, the ancient world was chronically immoral. Society had become depraved and unbelievably corrupt. The pagan practices of Israel's contemporaries were too pornographic to be described in a book like this. Sexual promiscuity and every kind of perversion were commonplace. Yet living as they were within this vile world, God brought to his people this commandment: *No adultery!*

The same was true of New Testament times. Paul wrote letters to the infant church in Corinth, a city proverbial for its moral depravity. Right up to the middle ages, to call someone a 'Corinthian' was to imply he or she was an immoral slut. But yet Paul, building uncompromisingly on the standards of the Old Testament, challenged those who professed faith in Christ to adopt a morality which was in astonishing contrast to the hyper-permissiveness of first-century Corinth (1 Cor. 6).

Are we Christians today not in just the same situation as those Hebrew people in the midst of a wicked world? God commands us, as he did them, *No adultery!* Are we not increasingly in a similar moral climate to those early Christians, living in a

116

foul swamp of moral pollution? We too are likewise being exhorted and instructed in a pure and godly morality. The lower standards fall, the more relevant this seventh commandment becomes. The blacker the sky, the brighter the star. The more glowering the clouds, the more beautiful the rainbow. The darker the night, the clearer the light to show us the right path. *You shall not commit adultery.*

Christian marriage

Adultery is unthinkable for the Christian for many reasons. I want us to notice three in particular. The first is because of the Bible's clear stance on marriage. In teaching chastity outside marriage, the Lord goes right back to Genesis 2:24 for the divine principle: *For this reason a man will leave his father and his mother and be united to his wife, and they will become one flesh.* The Apostle Paul follows the Lord exactly in his position on marriage, and says the same: *For it is said, 'The two will become one flesh'* (1 Cor. 6:16).

Our Bible is consistent in the view of marriage it takes. It shows us that God's purpose is that the marriage relationship should be a complete union of mind, spirit and body. The physical union is never an end in itself. It seals and symbolises the far deeper union of two personalities joined together in marriage – a union that is intended by God to last a lifetime. As we have just seen, our Lord affirms this and the later New Testament writers confirm it, beyond any shadow of doubt in their teaching.

We are all aware of the massive assault today on this declared purpose of God. We know that many voices are urging that casual sexual liaisons outwith marriage are acceptable in our modern society. It comes at us from every side. A parent confided in me quite recently that a teenage magazine which had found its way into their home quite explicitly commended and advised on full sexual relationships between school pupils. Other teenage magazines (and some readers, without realising it, may well have adolescent children in possession of just such material), provide telephone numbers to call for lengthy descriptions of the techniques of oral sex and how to get the most out of it.

For all that, the standards of God cannot change, whatever the world may be saying to us and our teenagers. God's design and will are crystal clear. A man and woman are to be joined together within marriage alone, and that bond is for 'as long as they both shall live'.

The body
Second, immorality is unthinkable for the Christian because of the Bible's view of our bodies. Some religions make a distinction between the body and the spirit. Hinduism, for example, is dualistic in that way. Therefore in yoga the aim is not just to relax (as some naive people think), but by

118

meditation to separate the spirit from the body. The body is seen as evil, while the spirit is seen as good.

However, that kind of simplistic dualism is quite foreign to the biblical teaching on the body. The Christian faith insists on the essential unity of body, mind and spirit. Our bodies are not evil. They are created to be temples of the Holy Spirit. Three times in 1 Corinthians 6 Paul asks, *Do you not know?* and on each occasion he is emphasising the sanctity of the believer's body.

Because of this essential unity of body, mind and spirit, immorality is a sin against the whole personality. It is a deadly strike against the total man, the total woman. Immorality is a deep wound inflicted on mind and spirit, as well as a defilement that stains the body. It is a crime against the person.

The lie is abroad today that a little immorality does no harm. How false! Immorality seriously demeans the glory of a man and woman, created in the image of God, with bodies intended to be joined in lifelong union. And when the conscience ceases to cry out and adulterers wipe their hands and say, 'We have done no harm', then great injury has been done to their whole persons which no washing will cleanse. I have witnessed the anguished hearts of young women who discovered abortion could never take away their shame.

Forgiveness
The glorious truth is that there is a fountain for sin and all uncleanness. Those who turn with real

repentance and brokenness of spirit to the Lord can receive and experience his forgiveness. In the Bible, after David had committed adultery, he prayed, *Cleanse me with hyssop and I shall be clean; wash me, and I shall be whiter than snow.... Create in me a pure heart, O God, and renew a right spirit within me* (Ps. 51:7, 10). With that washing, the joy of salvation was restored to David. It can be the same for men and women today. If your conscience has similar deep stains and wounds, then read for yourself Psalm 51 which was written by a believer who repented and found cleansing from this very sin.

Slaves of Christ

We now go on to note a third reason why immorality is unthinkable for a Christian. It is because of the Christian's relationship to God.

In the first-century world when the New Testament was written, slaves could be set free by a custom known as 'sacral manumission'. That meant a relative could pay into the temple treasury of one of the Greek gods a ransom price for the slave. The slave in theory then became the slave of the god, but in practice that meant he or she was now free.

The apostle Paul wrote in exactly these terms, 'The Saviour has bought you.' *You are not your own, you were bought at a price* (1 Cor. 6:19f). His choice of words suggests he is using the custom of sacral manumission to illustrate the Christian's freedom. We were once slaves to passion, impurity, and even to fornication and adultery. But Christ has paid the price for us, and that price was his own life-blood. Therefore, *we are not our own, we were bought at a price.*

That must mean that we who belong to Christ are under a lifelong obligation to glorify Christ in our bodies. The Christian is a slave of Jesus Christ. We are his to serve, his to obey. Therefore for those of us who are Christians, our bodies must be daily surrendered to our Master, and never given over to immorality of any kind.

Temples of the Holy Spirit

You may recollect from your Sunday School or Bible Class days that the Tent of Meeting used for worship in the wilderness wanderings comprised three main areas. There was the outer court, where all worshippers could go. There was also the Holy Place where only the priests might go. Then there was the third area comprising the Holy of Holies, the inner sanctuary, where only the High Priest could go once a year on the Day of Atonement, that holiest of days in the Jewish calendar. It was in this inner sanctuary of the Holy of Holies that the Ark of the Covenant rested, in which the Ten Commandments were kept, and it was from there that the Shekinah Glory of God emanated.

In the same verse quoted above (1 Cor. 6:19), Paul writes: *Do you not know that your body is a temple of the Holy Spirit who is in you, whom you have received from God?* It is important to notice that his word for 'temple' means the 'inner shrine' of the Holy of Holies.

We sometimes say to the children (and with a degree of truth), that they must invite Jesus into their hearts. But Paul says something rather different here. He states that the Holy Spirit comes, not merely into our hearts, but also into our bodies. The Spirit makes his holy dwelling in our hands and feet, in our flesh and blood – in all of our 'members' and that takes in our bodies!

I recall a family in one of my previous parishes. Talk about 'airs and graces'! They expected, and everyone gave them, an elevated position in the community. Until something happened which brought the public view of them into a very different perspective. Quite innocently and during a church event in which their home was being used, two women found their way into this family's kitchen and uncovered a can of worms – literally! The kitchen's cutlery drawer was so filthy that it was crawling with maggots – all over the knives, forks and spoons. The rest of the kitchen was pretty much the same. One of the women was physically sick.

That is something of the reaction of the apostle Paul to the suggestion of immorality in a Christian. 'Unthinkable!' he says. 'Christians' bodies must be clean and pure, for they are the inner shrines in which the Holy Spirit makes his dwelling.'

Glorious bodies

In this day of dark cynicism, Christians are to be marked out by a glorious hope, the hope of the consummation of the Kingdom of God. On that final day of eternal resurrection, the believer will be given a new body, a glorious body, like the Lord's new body after his resurrection.

There was a common saying in Corinth, *Food for the stomach, and the stomach for food* (1 Cor. 6:13). The flow of Paul's argument and logic implies that this same principle was being applied to the sexual functions of the body, meaning that the sexual desires were there to be indulged to the full. 'It's only natural', was the argument. We have exactly the same argument today, only those who use it apparently have neither the wit nor the knowledge to know it is over 2,000 years old, and leads to degradation and depravity, the way it did in first-century Corinth.

'Wrong', retorts Paul. 'The body is not meant for sexual licence. It is meant for the Lord, who one day will change it to be like his glorious body.' We are to see him face to face, and since we have that hope, we purify ourselves, as Christ is pure (1 John 3:1ff). We are preparing our minds, spirits and *bodies* for eternity in the presence of God and his Son. (Of course, let it be understood that Paul holds that sexual fulfilment is one of God's gracious gifts to men and women. He never lays down that sex is wrong, only that sexual activity should be within the security of marriage.)

All this – that we are slaves of Christ, therefore our bodies do not belong to us but to Christ, that our bodies are the inner shrine where the Spirit dwells, and that our bodies are to be changed to be like Christ's resurrection body – all this adds up to the most powerful argument that obedience to the seventh commandment is the only option for the Christian, and that deviation from it is a most grievous sin.

Caught in the act

There was a woman who was caught in the act of adultery. Some who read this book may never have been caught in the act as she was, but may still be secretly guilty of breaking the seventh commandment. To such Christ's words still come: *Neither do I condemn you* (to the death by stoning), *go and sin no more* (John 8:11). 'His blood can make the foulest clean, his blood avails for me.'

A particular temptation

Many years ago, I was sitting relaxing at a social evening in the home of a Christian man I greatly admired. During the conversation, the subject came up of a sin which I had been myself sorely tempted to commit. My friend spoke of this particular sin with contemptuous disgust. I felt very ashamed, and trembled at what he would think of me if only he knew how I had sometimes felt!

Later on that same evening, my friend spoke of another quite different sin which he and his brother had indulged in as teenagers. He regaled the company with an amusing account of what they had done, and everyone laughed hilariously at the daring of the brothers in their youth years before. However it so happened that the sin which the brothers had committed was one which filled me with contemptuous disgust, so I couldn't join in the laughter for I was quite shocked.

I learned something important that evening. I learned that one person's strength may well be another person's weakness. I learned that I must not condemn someone who is tempted severely in ways I might never have been tempted.

Many readers may never have been tempted to break the seventh commandment. But there will be some who have been tempted in this way in the past and will be so tempted in the future. I want, therefore, to suggest four ways in which we may be strengthened in our resolve to withstand this particular temptation.

A clean mind
We must allow no immorality in our thinking. In his Sermon on the Mount, the Lord said, *You have heard that it was said, 'You shall not commit adultery'. But I tell you, whoever looks lustfully has already committed adultery in his heart* (Matt. 5:27f). The Lord traces this sin back to its birth – a temptation in the mind, but a temptation which is allowed to linger, and is fed, enjoyed and mentally indulged.

We all know how such thoughts can be triggered. We read scandal in the newspapers, and find ourselves enjoying the sins of others – so we even sin by proxy in our thoughts. We watch a programme on television, and the seed is sown in our thoughts by what we see. Or we browse through a magazine, and there paraded before us is blatant immorality.

Here, then, is where the battle must be fought and won first of all – in our minds. Paul wrote, *Take every thought captive to obey Christ* (2 Cor. 10:5). The society we live in makes this very difficult. We are deluged every day by unclean images and suggestions. We are assured that, since everyone else is doing it, it must be all right. The assault is on our minds, and it can be a sore battle to fight because the smouldering embers of our old sinful natures are quickly fanned into a blaze by the devil as he works his bellows on our imaginations and into our desires. It only needs the dry sticks of circumstances to be gathered together, and the tinder of opportunity to be struck, for an unholy conflagration to be kindled which can quickly set on fire our whole lives, and reduce to ashes all we have spent years in building. How often have we seen the bitter fruits of yielding to this temptation, not just in the lives of those who have fallen, but also in the lives of many others who became entangled in the deadly web woven by infidelity.

So those who are tempted to sin must constantly fight the battle of the mind. 'God be in my head, and in my understanding.' Not only pray Christ to keep your mind; also guard yourself with vigilance as well.

Holy fear

A second weapon against immorality is fear of God. I am not thinking of a slavish, cringing fear such as a dog shows towards a brutal master. There is a loving, filial fear. 'Oh how I fear thee living God, with deepest, tenderest fears...'

Those who do not know the Lord can be over-influenced by silly, childish fears. They can be too concerned about what the neighbours will think. Or about what their colleagues at work might say. 'Just say such-and-such happens, what will I do then?' they constantly wonder. In sharp contrast to such an attitude, the Christian must fear the Lord. We must fear lest we grieve him and his Holy Spirit be taken from us. *Do not take your Holy Spirit from me,* prayed David (Ps. 51:11). We must fear lest our fellowship with our Saviour be broken. Isaiah wrote, *Do not fear what they fear, do not dread it. The Lord of Hosts you are to regard as holy, he is the one you are to fear* (Isa. 8:12). While perfect love casts out fear, we must still fear God!

Remember how Joseph was persistently tempted by Potiphar's wife. Joseph's reply to her stands for all time as an example of holy fear: *How can I do this wickedness and sin against God?* (Gen. 39:9). Because Joseph feared the Lord, he was preserved. That fear of God, said Bernard of

Clairveaux, is *janitor animae* – 'the doorkeeper of the heart'.

Avoid idleness

A third way to guard against immorality is to avoid idleness. It was when David was idle that he was tempted. He had become soft and self-indulgent. As a result his home was wrecked and his kingdom torn from him by his own son. His sin with Bathsheba was easily traceable to idleness. (The connection between David's adultery and Absalom's rebellion is not difficult to trace. You can follow the sad train of events as the king failed to deal with Amnon – he had been guilty of a similar sin himself – so that Absalom took matters into his own hands and then went unforgiven by his father. The break in their relationship ultimately led to rebellion and the deepest of suffering for the whole nation as well as for David. See 2 Samuel 11-19.)

Today, technology has brought increased leisure to some. But the habits and pleasures of leisure can hold great snares. The modern fashion of wining and dining often goes with lax manners which ignore the old conventions of respect for the dignity of the opposite sex. When such laxity is taken for granted, then guards can be dropped, and temptation has a far easier entrance.

I am reliably informed that each person's sexual drive is in direct proportion to his or her capacity for work. In the church of God, there ought to be no unemployment. The need is great. Workers for the kingdom are urgently wanted. So let us avoid idleness and direct our energies unceasingly into Christ's royal service.

Purest love

Perhaps the most powerful safeguard against the temptation to violate this seventh commandment is love itself. To those who are married I must say, love your beloved so fiercely and so strongly that anything which dares to come between you is mercilessly put to death at once. To love one's partner (or, if you are single, to love those whom Christ asks you to love for his sake), is the greatest defence of all against immorality. By love, I don't mean mere romance (though few wives will complain if their husbands keep plenty of romance in their marriages). Real love is enduring, tough, sacrificial.

There are certain doors in our lives which should never ever be reopened after marriage. Once the vows have been made, the keys of those doors should be turned in the locks and then destroyed. The trouble with too many marriages today is that a few months after marriage, certain doors are secretly and deliberately opened – just a little. How can there be a secure, lasting relationship when the possibility of ending the marriage is even allowed to be treated as an option? The battle is lost almost before it is started.

Men, be infatuated with the love of your wives.

Cherish them, adore them. That is the commandment of God. Wives, be gentle and respectful towards your husbands, honouring them, encouraging and nurturing their love for you.

Those who have no marriage partner, there is a whole world that desperately needs your love. There are boys and girls who need an enduring, tough, sacrificial love. There are young people, elderly, others with special needs, who are looking for your love. Our world is starved of pure, holy, righteous love.

The ultimate model of love for all of us is our Lord himself. Are we experiencing each day the depths of his tenderness and faithfulness, his enduring, sacrificial and lavish love? Yet, how often is our relationship with Christ marred by our laxity and infidelity? In spite of all our unfaithfulness, he remains faithful. His covenant love calls us to return to him, that he might freely and fully restore us to himself: *I will heal their faithlessness; I will love them freely ... they shall return and live beneath my shadow, they shall flourish as a garden, they shall blossom as the vine* (Hos. 14:4ff).

The
Eighth
Commandment

You shall not steal (Exod. 20:15).

Zacchaeus said, 'If I have defrauded anyone of anything, I restore it fourfold.' Jesus said, 'Today salvation has come to this house' (Luke 19:8-9).

A national newspaper recently published a Board of Trade estimate that over 13% of our Gross National Product is stolen every year. Those involved range from top management to humblest cleaner. In the building industry alone, enough materials go 'missing' annually to build a fair-sized town. The eighth commandment says, 'You shall not steal'!

I had an idle moment to think about this law. My thoughts wandered round the room, and settled on the bookshelf. I found my eye resting on a forgotten volume I had borrowed years ago ... I worked it out – twelve years ago! Then I saw another and another.... Surely, Lord, I haven't STOLEN them?

The commandment murmurs, 'You shall not steal.'

Through in the kitchen, while filling the kettle to make a cuppa, I remembered that when the house was built, the contractor forgot to include the handsome 'mixer-tap' in the final account. I never raised it with him. After all, it's his responsibility, not mine, to keep track of work he does. I would have paid for it, had I been asked. Surely, Lord, I have not stolen it?

The commandment whispers, 'You shall not steal.'

Slipping into the garage to put a tool away, I saw a box of screws staring at me. I wondered why I felt guilty. Then I recalled that a tradesman had left them behind: 'They'll never be missed,' he had said, 'you just keep them'. But they were not his to give, nor mine to keep. Surely Lord, I did not steal them?

The commandment still insists, 'You shall not steal.'

Lord! Where do I draw the line? These envelopes from the office ... the paper ... drawing pins ... the personal call on my boss's phone in my boss's time ... it's becoming absurd, ridiculous! No one bothers about trivia like this nowadays. It's accepted, Lord, that we help ourselves a little, here and there.

My child, My Holy Spirit is the Spirit of Truth. He is pleased to live in a life that is transparently honest, with no shadow of deceit; no grey areas. God is light, and in Him is no darkness at all. Repay what is owed. Return what is not yours. Then salvation will have come to your house!

The Eighth Commandment
No Theft!

You shall not steal (Exod. 20:15).

Every Chancellor of the Exchequer strives to grasp for his party and the country the golden apple of prosperity. The struggle is ongoing, against inflation on the one hand, and recession on the other hand. The theory is that a growing economy will keep the electorate happy and will ensure another term of office for the party at the next election. Yet there is one single measure which, though it lies beyond the ability of any Chancellor to deliver, would have power to change the course of our United Kingdom's economic fortunes. It can be summed up in four monosyllabic words: *You shall not steal.*

Almost every business in the land suffers from theft. The supermarkets have to impose a surcharge of about five or six percent on everything we buy to cover losses from shoplifting. Public transport costs are high because so many dodge paying fares. Every day, in spite of closed circuit cameras, motorists drive out of filling stations without paying for their petrol. Tools disappear from workshops; materials are stolen from building sites; cutlery from restaurants; bed sheets from hospitals – the loss to the National Health Service from theft runs to millions each year! The list is seemingly endless.

The effect of theft on the population is all-pervasive: the cost of daily living is greatly increased as prices honest people pay are constantly raised to cover the losses of theft. It is reckoned by economists that over thirteen percent of our gross national product is stolen every year. If people obeyed this eighth commandment, national productivity would leap by a massive thirteen percent, instead of by the paltry one or two percent for which successive chancellors work and plan.

Stealing from our neighbours

I want to divide our thinking into two main parts. The first concerns the way in which we can steal from our neighbours. The second is directed towards ways in which it is possible for us to steal from God himself.

Employer and employee

The Levitical code of laws was very pointed in its concern to protect the employee from the unscrupulous employer. *Do not take advantage of a hired worker ... pay him his wages ... lest he cry to the Lord and it be a sin in you* (Deut. 24:14ff). That takes in so much. Not only does it take in cheating an employee out of his wages, it also includes paying him too little or delaying giving him what he has earned. All these fall within the orbit of the eighth commandment, and are therefore sins against God. (Note that in my treatment of this commandment, I am following John Calvin in taking the Levitical laws as an exposition of the Ten Commandments.)

Conversely, an employee can steal from the employer. Failing to work conscientiously during the hours for which one is paid is theft. Arriving at work late or leaving early is also theft. Attending to personal business during working hours may well be theft. Making personal calls on the company telephone without permission is theft. *You shall not steal* – from your employer. *You shall not steal* – from your employee. If a fair day's pay was always given for a fair day's work, and if a fair day's work was always given for a fair day's pay, there can be no doubt that our country's economy would be transformed.

Dealings in the business world
However, work and pay are only the tip of the iceberg in any national economy. The Old Testament laws were well aware of that, and so the amplification of the eighth commandment included business dealings. *You must have accurate and honest weights and measures, so that you may live long in the land the Lord your God is giving you* (Deut. 25:13-16). We have referred already to the immense problem of theft by shoplifting. But there can be the most subtle theft by suppliers too.

We are surrounded by deceit and

136

misinformation. The skills of modern psychology have been used to persuade the consumer to believe many lies. The old pound jar was first replaced by a twelve ounce jar which was carefully designed to look rather like a pound jar. But it was shaped to hold twenty-five percent less. I know the quantities are printed on the label, but many a busy housewife or trusting pensioner was deceived, and I suggest that was exactly the intention. The move from the imperial system of weights and measures to metric has also provided suppliers with ample opportunity to practise the same kind of deceit.

We are offered some new washing powder, and the advertising commercial shows a supposed test which proves a new formula works wonders on blackcurrant stains. But very often the whole exercise is riddled with deception and is based on 'economy with the truth'. Nevertheless, the success or otherwise of the television commercial consists in persuading viewers of the complete 'honesty' of the housewife who is portrayed as discovering this new product has done the seemingly impossible.

No matter how often legislation is introduced to prevent this kind of dishonesty, the ingenuity of the advertisers' minds finds a way round the law to deceive the public again and disregard this eighth commandment. Vast sums of money are spent on producing these television commercials. Brilliant minds are stretched to the limit in the deliberate effort to deceive. Therefore the commandment is broken in the intention of the advertisement, if not in the letter of government legislation.

Dealings with the poor

In Hebrew society, if someone was poor, and with little or no resources was struggling to get on to his feet, Moses laid down that he was to be given an interest-free loan (Exod. 22:25; Lev. 25:35ff). This was perhaps an unexpected law, providing help for the poor at the expense of the better-off. This provision is greatly strengthened because the Levitical law states that to charge the poor with interest is to rob them for this simple reason that they cannot afford to pay interest.

I wonder if we all realise that in our generation as we in Europe and America go about our daily business, western banks are charging Third World countries enormous sums of money in interest for financial assistance given. It is hardly surprising that the circle is now being completed as the wealthy banks are discovering to their loss that any chance of ever seeing their money repaid is only a remote possibility.

The truth of the matter is that while we have been giving help with one hand, we have been robbing the Third World with the other as for years our banks have been pulling back in interest payments massive sums of money which these nations simply could not afford. According to the Christian Bible, this has been a violation of the eighth commandment.

An extension of this very humanitarian measure was the provision in Moses' elucidation of the eighth commandment that when someone became bankrupt, his creditors might not take away everything he owned. Nor might they force an eviction to seize goods and property (Deut. 24:10ff). Only what he possessed in excess of reasonable daily requirements could be taken from the bankrupt. God's law was full of compassion and plain humanitarian common sense.

Stealing apples from an orchard

In the Mosaic law, it isn't apples, of course, it is grapes. The law was this. It was not stealing to help yourself from someone else's crop as long as you ate there and then what you took. You could not carry fruit away with you (Deut. 23:24f). Therefore, if you were travelling and ran out of food, by law you could enter someone's garden or orchard or vineyard, help yourself and have a snack on the spot.

How very sensible! No need for children to make raids on the neighbour's apple trees. Few children can eat more than one apple at a time, anyway. However, if a thief was caught carrying away someone's crop, the corporal punishment administered would have been very painful, whatever the European Court of Human Rights might say about it.

Lost property and bribes

Two other provisions we should notice. The old saying does not hold true in biblical law, 'Finders keepers', or as they say in the locality where I come from, 'He that finds keeps, he that loses greets' ('greets' means 'cries'). Lost property had to be restored. If the owner was unknown, the goods had to be kept safe until the true owner was identified (Deut. 22:2f).

Moreover, bribes to secure business or to influence a decision were forbidden. They were seen as another violation of the eighth commandment. (Exod. 23:6ff, and see Prov. 15:27). Yet in our society today bribery is becoming increasingly common. The heritage of our Christian tradition is being lost as 'sleaze' is creeping in at every level of commerce and industry. I constantly ask myself if people today realise what they are rejecting when they turn their backs on God and his word.

The principle of restitution

If a theft was committed and the thief caught, then not only did he have to restore what he had stolen, but he also had to add on as much again to compensate for the distress, inconvenience, loss of profit, and waste of time caused by his dishonesty. In certain circumstances, the rate of restitution was five hundred percent, but usually, it was repayment at the rate of two hundred percent (Exod. 22:1ff). For example, if a sheep was stolen then the price of two sheep must be paid back in restitution. Or to bring the law into our terms, if £100 had been stolen £200 had to be paid back. If the loss was entirely through accidental damage, then full restitution had to be made plus a surcharge of twenty percent to compensate for any inconvenience caused. This principle of restitution was writ large in the Mosaic laws.

Why has this simple principle been abandoned by our penal system? Let me give you a personal example. A number of years ago, one of our children went to a local shop to buy some item for my wife. The child was mugged by three boys and the family housekeeping purse was stolen. The police quickly caught the offenders and recovered the purse, by which time it was empty, needless to say. The police insisted on keeping the purse as evidence. We never saw it again, and no restitution was ever made. I would suggest that if the Mosaic law had been followed, and those boys' parents had been ordered to repay at least double the amount their sons had stolen, they might have taken more interest in what the boys were up to from then on.

I have a journalist friend who for years lived and worked in Edinburgh. She told me that in 1956, after the Billy Graham Crusade in the Kelvin Hall in Glasgow, stories poured into all the newspaper offices about restitution being made. People turned up at stores to pay for goods they had stolen, often years before. Bills that had been overlooked through clerical errors were asked for so that full payment could be made. Shoplifters who had been converted to Christ returned stolen goods. It was like a dream for several months as people all over central Scotland put right the dishonesty of past years. It is interesting to notice that such acts of restitution have often accompanied the work of the Holy Spirit in those who have come to a living faith in Christ. Without ever having been taught this provision of the biblical laws, a fruit of the new divine nature within them has instructed them to make full restitution.

There are examples of this in Scripture. Remember the story of Zacchaeus. Christ came into his life, so certain matters had to be put right. His conscience was re-educated by the Holy Spirit. Thus his years of dishonesty were dealt with, and he proceeded to pay back double the rate prescribed by Moses' law. Instead of two hundred per cent, he paid back four fold of all that he had stolen.

I recall leading a man to Christ some years ago after an evening service which he had attended in the church where I was then minister. Up to that point, he had for two years been making false claims for payments from social security. The first thing he did next morning was to go and put right what was wrong. He went and made a full confession of dishonesty that had been a way of life for years. It cost him dear. But by midday, it had all been dealt with.

If Jesus Christ was to go through some of our

homes, our tool sheds, our bank accounts, our places of work, Christ, whose eyes are like flames of fire, seeing all, knowing all, I wonder what he might have to say to some of us. I wonder if his finger would stop at any page on our tax form? I wonder if his hand would touch any item or article in our home? I wonder if he would say to some readers, 'I must have truth and righteousness in the inward heart; until you set that matter right, you have no part with me.'

Have any sins of dishonesty or misappropriation come between us and our God? Is our attendance at our churches an act of hypocrisy, because we are knowingly and deliberately allowing violation of the spirit of this commandment in our lives? We cannot worship God with sin in our lives. *If I cherish iniquity in my heart, the Lord does not hear me* (Ps. 66:18).

God is not primarily concerned with how well-turned out we are, or what good citizens we appear to be. It was when Zacchaeus began to hand back what he had taken – and I'm sure he often said to himself, 'All tax-collectors do this!' – and then to give away half his great wealth, it was then that Christ said, *Today, salvation has come to this house* (Luke 19:9).

You shall not steal from God
The prophet Malachi asked a most unexpected question: *Will a man rob God? Yet you rob Me.* The people replied, *How do we rob God?* The

answer came, *In tithes and offerings. You are under a curse the whole nation of you – because you are robbing Me* (Mal. 3:8ff).

The tithe is one tenth, ten percent. The people were asked to give one tenth of their total income to God, for the upkeep of God's House, for the support of the priesthood, and for the continuance of God's work. In Malachi's day, there was a severe recession. Times were hard. The people were taking the line that they could no longer afford to give the tithe to God, far less the offerings on top of the tithe. (Incidentally, notice that when the Lord spoke about our generosity being confidential, *Let not your right hand know what your left hand is doing,* he was referring to what was given over and above the tithe and the three days' pay towards the fabric of the temple [the half-shekel temple tax]. It was what was given over and above these two charges on each Jew's income that was to remain absolutely confidential.)

Deception

Not everyone agrees that one tenth is a proper amount to give to God. I know that many readers and tens of thousands of professing Christians disagree with that level of giving laid down in the Bible. How do I know? The reason is very obvious. It is that the average givings in most congregations fall far, far below what they would be if only half of the members were tithing their income. If the Lord's people all believed in and practised tithing, it would mean the average income of the adult members of most Christian congregations would be somewhere around £25 a week. Clearly, that is not so. The national average is many times higher than that. Therefore it is self-evident that only a few in our churches today take God's word seriously. The claims we make with our lips are denied by our actions.

The situation is actually worse than that. Some years ago I spoke to my congregation about the low level of our giving (as I saw it) and was quickly told that many members were giving sacrificially towards the support of the two missionaries who had gone out from the fellowship. A few months later, the opportunity came my way to check on how much support was being given privately for these two missionaries from the county in which our congregation was situated and it transpired an extremely small amount was being given by one single person. So some of my members deliberately had falsely given me to understand their level of giving to the church was low because they were sending money to the Lord's work elsewhere. They hid their disobedience to God's word by telling lies, and these were professing evangelical Christians.

Let's face it. Whatever reasons we give, and I know that many Christian people do support other Christian work independently of what they give to the Lord's work in their church, the truth is that many, many are today robbing God. *Will a man rob God? Yet you rob Me,* says the Lord. But you ask, *How do we rob God?* The answer comes back, *In tithes and offerings ... the whole nation of you are robbing me.* The result is that God's work in many places languishes through lack of funds.

Spiritual theft

Would we rob our butcher or our grocer, our milkman or our newsagent? Would we go for months and years with bills unpaid? What would happen if we did? Then why rob the Lord? For one of two reasons. Either we are so much in love with the fleeting things of this life that we love them more than we love God. Or else we simply do not love the Lord enough to obey His word. There can be no other reasons that I can think of.

I know all the arguments for not giving one tenth of our incomes to God. For ten years I was in the ministry on the minimum stipend, living in a vast draughty Victorian manse with fourteen rooms that we couldn't afford to heat. We had three growing children whom we dressed out of jumble sales because we couldn't afford to buy them new clothes. We certainly couldn't afford a luxury such as a newspaper, far less a television. For the first twenty years of married life the only holiday we could afford was to go to stay with in-laws. Regularly we went to bed hungry at night.

It was while we were on that level of income that God asked me this question, *Will a man rob God?* After an intense personal struggle, I began to deduct from my pay cheque as the very first

146

charge the full tithe and give it to God. I know the cost of doing that. But I also have learned the joy of bringing to God as a minimum the tenth he requires in order that his work may prosper, the hungry be fed, the naked clothed and the poor have the Gospel preached to them. *Will a man rob God?* You shall not steal.

Promises of blessing
It would be unfaithfulness on my part not to underline the promises that God gives us about his response when his people tithe. In Malachi 3:10ff, we read, *Bring the whole tithe into the storehouse ... Test me in this, says the Lord of Hosts, and see if I will not throw open the floodgates of heaven and pour out so much blessing that you will not have room enough for it. Then all nations will call you blessed....*

Now we have to be careful at this point. It is not that when we give our tithes to God a kind of mechanical law comes into operation and God blesses in return. Not that at all. There is never anything mechanical or automatic about spiritual things. The principle is quite different. Rather is it that when our hearts are right with God, and when material things are given second place – because, note, God is given *first* place – then when we have enthroned the Lord in our hearts, God blesses us as he promises.

It is all a matter of our hearts and of who or what is our God. When God is truly our Lord, to obey his commandments will be a delight, for he writes them on our hearts. Then written on our hearts is: You shall not steal, either from your neighbour or from your God.

The
Ninth
Commandment

You shall not bear false witness (Exod. 20:16).

God is light and in Him is no darkness at all (1 John 1:5).

Grace and truth came through Jesus Christ (John 1:17).

The Ten Commandments all reflect something of the revealed nature of God. The ninth commandment is concerned with His love for truth.

Lord God, Your nature is light, and You love the truth. You see everything there is to see; and You know those secrets of our lives that are ugly and shameful, things we often find hard to admit to ourselves. We are amazed, Lord, that in spite of all You see and know, You love us still.

Lord Jesus, You came to bring to us the truth of the Father. Your teaching words, Your healing actions, and Your redeeming work combine to make crystal clear Your radiant truth – the truth about Your holiness, the truth about Your mercy, the truth about Your love. In You, grace and truth join hands, and You welcome and embrace us, sinners though we are.

Spirit of Truth, Your gentle work is to take the truth as it is in Jesus, and apply it to our lives. Bring us to love the truth. Give us hearts that abhor all that is dark, deceitful, dishonest. Lead us in those pathways of transparent living, where there is no shadow of false speaking, no game of pretending, no cloak of hypocrisy. Direct us in the paths of righteousness, where truth is spoken and lived in love.

The Ninth Commandment
Truthfulness

You shall not give false testimony
against your neighbour (Exod. 20:16).

We have learned to excuse a large variety of sins,
and to call them by other names. For example, we
speak about something having 'fallen off the back
of a lorry' but we are really talking about stolen
goods. Or we speak about a little sex on the side
but that is a sly term for adultery. We may talk
about having a bit of fun but that can be a way of
saying alcohol has been seriously abused.

It's the same with lies and dishonesty. How
often we hear it said that there is a credibility gap
between a politician and the people. What we mean
is that he has told lies so often that no one any
longer believes a word he says. There is the famous
phrase from one of Margaret Thatcher's most loyal
servants who said he was being 'economical with
the truth'. Tell me what that means if it does not
mean he was deceiving the court where, as he was
giving testimony, he was withholding material
evidence.

However, the significant thing is that out of all
the sins condemned in the Ten Commandments,
the sin which the ninth commandment condemns
is the sin we least easily forgive. For no one loves
a liar. Once you've caught out a liar, you find it

hard to trust him again. How can you have a meaningful relationship with a liar? You can't really, can you?

Economic prosperity

Take this a little further. It would not be over-stating the case to say that the whole prosperity of any nation depends on truth being upheld within that nation. Do we realise that? It is a staggering statement. But any nation's economic and domestic prosperity can only be founded on truth and honesty.

You see, if the courts of a nation cannot be trusted to uphold the truth, and if that nation's banks and insurance companies cannot be relied upon to deal honestly with the money they hold, then people will neither do business with that country nor invest in its banks. In the past, this has been one of the sources of our own nation's wealth. Foreign investors knew their money would be safe. They knew that if the crunch ever came, the courts would act honestly, and the banks would repay their money.

Why is it so many of the Third World countries cannot climb out of their permanent state of poverty? Why will banks no longer lend to them? (This is a quite different issue from that we raised in the previous chapter about banks overcharging poor nations with high interest rates.) Why will foreign investors not risk their money with them? Because where there is corruption, bribery, chronic dishonesty and where men break their word, business cannot thrive. And the world, if the truth were told, hates a liar. So we must not think this ninth commandment is one of the least of the commandments of God. It is anything but that! Rather it is the cornerstone of society. Lose this, and we lose everything. Let us then take with the utmost seriousness this ninth commandment: You shall not give false testimony against your neighbour.

Truthfulness in the courts and public life

As with the other commandments, we find in the small print of the Mosaic legislation careful explanations of what is meant. *If a malicious witness takes the stand to accuse a man of a crime ... and if the witness proves to be a liar, giving false testimony ... then do to him as he intended to do to his brother ...* (Deut. 19:16ff). What does that mean? Take as an example someone who was 'framed' and falsely accused of sending a letter-bomb. Those who tried to frame him should, according to this law, receive the very sentence someone convicted of sending a letter-bomb would receive.

Honesty is given the very highest priority in the Bible's thinking, because without complete honesty, the framework of society begins to crumble. If we cannot trust the courts, or if we cannot trust those who work in the courts, then where can we turn? It becomes each one for him or herself, and we move into a twilight world where people with money, who are willing to pay, can get whatever they want.

Corruption in high places

We need to note this. In recent years in the United Kingdom, in the European Community and even in sport as high up as the international committee charged with choosing the host city for the Olympic Games, we have witnessed corruption. It has at times extended to the police and also to local government as well as to the highest levels of Parliament. Indeed, charges of sleaze against members of John Major's political party were undoubtedly a significant factor in bringing his government down in the 1997 General Election. That is a most ominous sign for any nation. We are in danger of moving into a post-Christian age in which we can no longer take for granted the most basic standards of integrity.

Investigate what happens in countries where there is no such integrity. Unfortunately, there are countries like that in the world today. What do we find? We discover no one is safe, the security of the common man has gone and life has become very dangerous. No one quite knows when a knock may come on the door or when a person may be falsely accused. Power lies in the hands of those with money, and corruption abounds. Some readers may have visited countries like that. One quickly realises that no one is safe, anything goes, bribery is rife and petty officials will rob a stranger without batting an eye.

Truthfulness in everyday living

We all know plenty about false statements in everyday living. We sometimes call it gossip, and the sad fact is that most of us will have indulged in gossip on some occasion in the past. It is a disease that poisons much of what is said. Often what we pass on to others is either hearsay or half-truth. The trouble with that is that it can be both unkind and unsavoury. Indeed, too often that is why we pass it on.

Any journalist will tell you that good news is not particularly interesting for newspaper editors. What they want is bad news or tragedy or scandal. People want to hear about the sordid, the unclean, the unworthy. It is part of the bentness of our fallen human natures. Therefore many of us pick up scraps of information and we pass them on with evident relish. Often that is done whether or not we are sure of the truth of what we are saying. The result is that both the characters of individuals and the reputations of whole families can be seriously damaged on evidence that could never stand in a court of law.

My own mother had a strict rule which she applied to all our conversation when we were children. She would want to know: 'Is it kind? Is it true? Is it necessary?' If she suspected any of us of indulging in gossip, she would immediately intervene and ask, 'Is it kind? Is it true? Is it necessary?' Only if what was being said passed the test of all three criteria could the conversation continue.

James in the third chapter of his letter reminds us how hard it is to tame the tongue. Lions, tigers, elephants and other wild beasts can be tamed and taught to obey. But no one can tame the tongue. It is full of deadly poison, and can act like a tinder which by one single spark can produce a great blaze. Indeed, it can set the whole course of nature on fire. One day our tongues are like sweet fountains yielding fresh, clean water, but the next day they are like stagnant ditches, full of bitter, infected, stinking water (See Jas. 3:1-12).

Every day, our tongues need to come under the cleansing of Christ, and the constraint of the Holy Spirit. I suppose that in the final analysis the love of Christ is the only really effective curb on what we say. That is why the whole of the Law and the Ten Commandments are summed up by the word 'Love'. If we love our God and our neighbour, then that love will be a gracious restraint on what we say.

Truthfulness in the Church

The Christians in the church at Corinth had been quarrelling. We are all human, and as long as we live in this old, fallen world with its imperfections, differences and problems will arise between us on account of misunderstandings and disagreements. However, not only were some of the Christians in Corinth disagreeing and quarrelling, some had even taken legal proceedings against their fellow-Christians. The technical term for this is 'litigation'. I have witnessed the way churches in some Third

World countries have been greatly damaged and weakened by such litigation between Christians.

The Apostle Paul was grieved to learn what was happening in Corinth, and so he addressed this problem (see 1 Cor. 6:1-8), giving reasons why no Christian should take another Christian to court. It will be worth noticing what Paul has to say since it has a practical bearing on the ninth commandment.

The family of God
First, Christians are brothers and sisters in the family of God. Is there not something odious about brothers fighting with each other in a court of law? Surely members of a family ought to be able to settle matters between themselves. Even more so should brothers and sisters in Christ be able to settle their differences within the church family.

Second, Paul points out that there are within the fellowship people of great wisdom: mature and godly elders appointed under the direction of the Holy Spirit. Quarrels, therefore, should be taken to these elders of the church, so that they can graciously and prayerfully advise and help the two sides to reach loving understanding.

Third, Christians have a bond with each other which those outside of Christ do not have. How dare they, then, take their differences to those who are outside that bond and who can never appreciate what their spiritual bond means. It is, argues Paul, completely wrong for believers to go with their disagreements to those who are outside of Christ.

Now while such litigation within Christian fellowships in our own land is highly unlikely, unfortunately the chances of more mundane, everyday disagreements and misunderstandings among Christians are almost inevitable. Paul was basing his counsel in this matter on the teaching of the Lord Jesus Himself. Here is what the Lord said (Matt. 18:15ff): *If your brother sins against you, go and show him his fault, just between the two of you.... But if he will not listen, take one or two others along, so that every matter may be established by the testimony of two or three witnesses. If he refuses to listen to them, tell it to the church: and if he refuses to listen even to the church, treat him as you would an outsider....*

How much heartache and bitterness would have been prevented if Christians had acted on the words of Christ! Even if step one had been taken, and the one with whom there had been a disagreement had been approached, at least ninety percent of misunderstandings would have been avoided. How very rarely would step two, that is, bringing the matter to one or two other members of the fellowship, have ever needed to be taken!

The Holy Spirit grieved
The tragedy is many churches are weakened, the Spirit grieved and his power quenched because such openness is lacking, with the result that misunderstandings grow, and begin to fester until ultimately the poison spreads through the whole body.

159

As well as broken relationships, consider also the unseen effects of such disagreements between believers. Think of the minister who spends whole days preparing for the services of the church each week. When most people are relaxing, or pursuing some hobby, or socialising with their friends, he is alone wrestling with his preparation, sweating it out. Then at the congregation's prayer gathering and during the week in the privacy of their homes, the committed Christians pray for God's presence and power upon the Word and among the congregation on the Lord's Day. Yet how often is the fire of God quenched and the Spirit of God grieved, because there are grudges and disagreements between members of the fellowship? Brothers and sisters in the family of God are clandestinely not speaking to each other, unable to forgive and harbouring grudges. Much of the sacrificial toil of the preacher and the prayers of the Lord's people are brought to nothing because the devil has gained a foothold through broken relationships.

The tragedy is made worse because often there is only one involved in the quarrel. Frequently the other party has been quite unaware of having done anything wrong. All that has been needed has been a forgiving spirit which is given when the blood of Christ cleanses our hearts. Of course it may be that two are involved, and a face to face encounter is needed, with a heart to heart exchange of deepest thoughts. How often has the blessing of God been withheld by the lack of that openness! In the history of revivals, we can see that at times the mighty power of God has fallen on the people of God only when the differences and misunderstandings have been cleansed away.

Truthfulness in God

Someone might be wondering what such disagreements and misunderstandings have to do with the ninth commandment. The answer is everything, because our God is the God of truth. To amplify what I mean, let's first consider briefly what our Bibles mean when they speak of 'truth'. What our Bibles mean by 'truth' and what we have therefore come to understand as 'truth' in our culture (which has been shaped in the past by Christian standards) is 'the real state of affairs', or 'what is actually the case'.

It may surprise some to learn that not every culture has such an understanding of truth. For example, in some countries in the Far East, truth is what people like to think might one day be the case. In these cultures, life in the past may have been harsh and cruel. Therefore the truth may at times also have been harsh and cruel. Having to face up to that was better avoided according to their way of thinking. Life would be much more bearable if one only thought and spoke as if everything was wonderful and desirable – even if that was in reality complete fiction.

Let me illustrate. Some forty years ago, I applied for a British Council scholarship to study in

Indonesia. While I would have been guaranteed an entry visa for myself had I been awarded the scholarship, my newly-wedded wife would not have been. There was no way I was going to go to Java for two years if the young lady I had just married could not go with me. So off we both went to the Indonesian Embassy in London to ask the cultural attaché there what the chances were of my wife also being given an entry visa.

We had two hours of frustrating conversation with an extremely polite and charming gentleman, in which all he would say was, 'By all means, let your wife apply for a visa', or, 'With all my heart, I hope your wife is granted a visa'. At last I cornered him into admitting that she would never be given a visa. But here is how he put it: 'I hope with all my heart that your beloved wife is the first ever student's wife to be granted an entry visa to my country.' You see, truth for the Indonesian was what he believed I would like to hear and what I was hoping to hear. What he said bore little or no relation to the real state of affairs.

Why is it, then, that in our western civilisations we insist that truth is the real state of affairs? Why do we identify truth with what is actually happening? As with so many other aspects of our western culture, we find the answer in our Old Testament Scriptures. We have learned from the Scriptures that God loves the truth. Truth is frequently personified as light. The God of light is all-seeing, and he knows the real state of affairs.

He sees what is actually happening. We cannot conceal anything from him for he sees and knows our hearts. *If I say, 'Surely the darkness will hide me and the light become night around me', even the darkness will not be dark to you; the night will shine like the day, for darkness is as light to you* (Ps. 139:11f).

We find that in the New Testament this same standard applies. John writes: *God is light, and in him there is no darkness at all* (1 John 1:5). We find Christ demanding that all forms of hypocrisy be purged from our living, for hypocrisy stands as the deadly enemy of the truth. The word 'hypocrite' comes from the language of the Greek theatre. Greek actors wore masks to help portray them as the characters they were acting. Therefore literally a hypocrite was someone who wore a mask to make him appear to be someone he was not. The hypocrite was a play-actor. The Lord spoke these terrible words: *Woe to you, teachers of the law and Pharisees, you hypocrites! You clean the outside of the cup and dish, but inside they are full of greed and self-indulgence. Blind Pharisee! First clean the inside of the cup and dish, and then the outside also will be clean* (Matt. 23:25ff.).

The hypocrite, you see, is only concerned with outward appearances. The hypocrite ignores the truth, the real state of affairs. Therefore the hypocrite falls foul of God, because God loves the truth. God is light and is concerned, not with what you and I may appear to be like to others, but with what we really are inside.

God is the God of truth and honesty. Pontius Pilate demanded with typical Roman scepticism, *What is truth?* Christ had said: *For this reason I was born, and for this I came into the world, to testify to the truth. Everyone on the side of truth listens to Me* (John 18:37f). John also tells us that the Lord was full of grace and truth (John 1:14). Those two qualities mingle perfectly in Christ, as in no one else. For he sees and knows the truth about you and me. He sees it all, the very worst. Nothing is hidden from his gaze. He, like no other, knows the real score about our characters. And yet, in his love, grace mingles with truth. Knowing the worst, his hand is still stretched out towards us, his forgiveness and mercy is still extended to us.

God's blessing and presence will be with those who love the truth, a people among whom there are no masks. He will be in that fellowship where truth is not only loved, but is also spoken in love. Dare we come and bow before the white light of God's all-seeing gaze? Dare we draw near to him whose eyes are as a flame of fire? As we come, dare we allow him to touch in our lives those things which need to be removed because they are incompatible with his love of truthfulness and honesty?

If we walk in the light, as he is in the light, we have fellowship one with another and the blood of Jesus Christ, his Son, cleanses us from all our sin (1 John 1:7). God demands truth in our inward being. Therefore, *You shall not give false testimony.*

164

The
Tenth
Commandment

You shall not covet (Exod. 20:17).

I should not have known what it is to covet if the law had not said, 'You shall not covet' (Rom. 7:7).

There is great gain in godliness with contentment (1 Tim. 6:6).

Happiness is the prize for which we all strive. But the great delusion is that happiness is to be achieved in 'getting'. Yet part of the sinfulness of humanity is that no matter how much we get, we are never satisfied, but always long for more. The tenth commandment opens our eyes to what is wrong, and directs our ways in what is right.

Lord, how hard to take seriously the poverty of so many in this world:
>children who are diseased and underfed,
>young people with no education, no employment, no prospects,
>families living in makeshift shelters built of materials gathered from the rubbish heaps,
– how hard, Lord, to take their poverty seriously!

Lord, how easy to let covetousness warp our thinking
>so that we look with envy on our neighbours,

on his new car, on her new microwave, on their
new home,
so that we believe that money really makes them
happy,
so that we forget that covetousness robs us of
our peace,
– how easy to be covetous, Lord!

Lord, how important to obey Your commandment:
to remember every day that You know all our
needs,
to realise that this world's goods are fleeting
and fading,
to live in that spiritual wealth of godliness with
contentment,
– how important, Lord, to keep our eyes on You!

*My child, during My earthly life, I owned no
wealth, no land, no home. Yet peace was always
Mine; Mine, not only to enjoy, but to share with
others. If only you, My people, would take Me
at My Word that happiness is not in getting,
but in giving.*

Lord, write Your word on my heart. Enable me to
take seriously the need of the world, the sin of my
greed, the truth of Your commandment. May I be
rich with that godly contentment which finds its
peace in You.

The Tenth Commandment
Covetousness

You shall not covet your neighbour's house. You shall not covet your neighbour's wife, or his manservant or maidservant, his ox or donkey, or anything that belongs to your neighbour
(Exod. 20.17).

We have all had the experience of meeting friends whom we haven't seen for years and being amazed at how much they have changed. They themselves are not so aware of the change, because they have lived with themselves and it's been a slow, imperceptible process. But we can be quite taken aback as we see how much they have altered.

I wonder if we realise that society is rather like that? People who return to this country after years abroad are amazed at the changes that have taken place. I don't just mean there are new shops, new roads, new houses. I mean there have been changes in attitude and outlook. We ourselves do not notice it, because the process of change has been gradual. However those who have been abroad for twenty years or so see it very clearly. They see a massive growth in materialism. They find that even with yet higher standards of living, people are still not content, but are still wanting more. Returning home from Third World countries as many of these exiles do, they see the dramatic difference in our standards of living compared to the dire poverty they have left behind. This shows up in an even worse light the discontent and greed which clamours for better conditions and more money.

I confess I know very little about economics but I do know that many in our country are inclined to look to America for an example. We see the huge commercial growth of America, and we want to copy their economic pattern. In real terms, the American Gross National Product has grown in fifty years from $1.5 trillion to nearly $6 trillion. It is a huge success story and we would like to emulate that kind of growth in prosperity.

Therefore successive chancellors, governments, and the official oppositions have all looked for growth – economic growth and prosperity. The aim is to put more money into people's pockets, to give them bigger and better houses, bigger and better cars, more consumer goods, longer holidays. These things apparently are what the electorate want more than anything else.

Look however at America! Just look! American society is very sick. The murder rate is far higher than it has ever been here in the United Kingdom, even higher than in Northern Ireland with all the political troubles and sectarian strife of past decades. The suicide rate in America is frightening. Drug trafficking is completely out of control. Marriage breakdowns are so frequent that there are special schools to cope with children whose parents have changed so often their family structure is like the proverbial Robert Bruce's axe which had had five new heads and seven new handles. American society is seriously sick.

We choose to ignore these facts. We ignore the huge demand in the States for psychiatric counselling. We ignore the millions of American teenagers on the open road as runaways from home. We ignore their astronomical crime rate. We ignore all of this because our greedy eyes are on their prosperity. Apparently, we would prefer material goods rather than a contented society with stable families. Crazy as it may seem, that appears to be how it is with us in these islands. That is exactly why the tenth commandment says: *You shall not covet....*

The meaning of covetousness

We read in the Gospels the incident of the rich young ruler who came to the Lord to ask the way to eternal life. The Lord answered: *You know the commandments...* and then quoted to him the fifth, sixth, seventh, eighth and ninth commandments. *Teacher,* the young man answered, *all these have I kept since I was a boy* (Mark 10:17ff). But the Lord knew that what he meant was that he had practised an outward, external obedience to the commandments. Outwardly, he had not stolen, murdered, committed an impure act, or disobeyed his parents.

It has been conclusively demonstrated that Saul

170

of Tarsus was studying under Gamaliel while Jesus was teaching in Jerusalem. Paul's statement in 2 Corinthians 5:16 is capable of being understood as saying that he had known the Lord during his earthly ministry. Therefore, the intriguing suggestion has been made that this rich young ruler was Saul of Tarsus. It is a fascinating suggestion because when Paul discusses the Ten Commandments in Romans 7, he says that while for years he had lived by the commandments in an outward, formal sense, their meaning had never penetrated the thick armour plating of his self-esteem. Like the young man in Mark 10, he thought he had never stolen, never dishonoured his parents, never given false witness, never been immoral. That is precisely the danger if we stop at the ninth commandment. We may have the boldness and blindness to dust ourselves down, glance admiringly at ourselves in the mirror of our self-righteousness, and tell ourselves we are not too bad.

It is a fact that so many who are regularly in the churches of our land do exactly that. We live in dangerous complacency, convinced we are fulfilling the law by doing our best. With the sweetest of smiles, and the darkest of hearts, so many say, 'I do no one any harm; I am trying my best.' That is just the night of ignorance, the trackless desert of spiritual lostness, in which the rich young ruler and Saul of Tarsus were wandering.

Reviving sin

It was when Saul (I am deliberately using his pre-Christian name) discovered this tenth commandment, *You shall not covet,* that the first grey light of the dawn of a new day began to dispel the darkness of his thinking. He tells us in Romans 7 that when he discovered this commandment, *sin revived and I died* (Rom. 7:7-10). Whatever does that mean – *sin revived and I died?* The first thing it means is that he began to see sin as it really is, not mere outward actions, but an inner condition of the soul.

This tenth command carried the divine law right into his very heart. It probed his most secret desires. It showed him that in spite of the correctness of his outward actions, God's concern was with the state of his heart. With a cry of anguish, he made the discovery that his Pharisee's strict life (you will remember Paul was a Pharisee before his conversion), was not the holy, upright life he imagined it to be, but was in reality corrupt, stained and twisted. This discovery all began with the tenth commandment which showed him that in his secret heart there was the greedy desire for more and more. That is what he means when he says the commandment, *You shall not covet,* caused sin to revive and him to die. The word of God smote and slew him.

As you have been reading through this book, we have been looking together at the Ten Commandments. My guess is that most readers will admit that many times the sword of God's word has wounded them deeply, opening up to them their hearts and showing them that they are transgressors of the law. But it may just be that some readers feel they have come this far unscathed. Right up to the tenth commandment you have held your head high and thought yourself an upright Christian, keeping all the commandments. I have to say unless this commandment shows us our sin (that is what it means by 'sin reviving'), and the light of God begins to dawn on us, we remain in the tragic darkness of thinking we are not condemned by the holy law of God.

The tenth commandment must show to us God's real concern never has been with what we think of ourselves, far less with what the neighbours may think. God never was a mere neighbour, peeping at us from behind the curtains. He is the holy God who sees our minds, our hearts, our desires.

Secret desires
In their exposition of the first nine commandments, the Puritans used to show how they were all inwardly violated because of this tenth commandment. The reason they gave was that it, more than all the others, directly addresses our inward, secret desires. In other words, the first nine commandments are all governed by the tenth commandment in that they are either obeyed or disobeyed within our hidden thoughts.

Sin revived and I died, Paul writes about the

impact this final commandment made on him after years of seeking to establish his own righteousness. For years, as Saul of Tarsus, the upright, correct, religious Pharisee, he had lived in the delusion that he was making the grade, earning his passage to heaven. Now the last of the commandments pierced his heart, and he saw that wrong desires were eating into and destroying his soul like a deadly dry rot. The truth was that for all his religion and good living he was a lost sinner, as far from pleasing God as the most hardened felon. At long last, all the commandments had done their faithful work in his life. This is why he goes on in Romans 7 to say: *So the law is holy, the commandment is holy and just and good.* It had awakened him to his desperate, urgent need of a Redeemer who could break the chains that bound him, a Saviour who could cleanse and forgive him.

Do you see, therefore, the importance of the tenth commandment? It shows us that covetousness expresses itself inwardly, even though our outward actions may be beyond reproach. It uncovers to us the real condition of our hearts.

The dangers of covetousness

I asked above if some who have been reading this little book which so far has sought to expound the first nine commandments, have comforted themselves that they are not too bad. 'We are alright. We haven't murdered, we haven't stolen, we don't worship false gods', you may have said.

174

But because the tenth commandment does not deal with outward actions, but with inner thoughts, it uncovers to us the deadly danger of covetousness. It shows us that here is a sin which our nearest and dearest may know nothing about, because it is concealed in the recesses of our hearts, unnoticed, undiscovered by those we meet every day.

I am sure many readers have walked through some of the delightful forest parks which are a feature of our countryside. You will have admired the fine trees you saw, and will have enjoyed passing under their overhanging branches and hearing the birds singing and calling across the woods. Recently I took such a walk. In the forest park I visited, I particularly noticed several trees which were in a dangerous condition. These trees were slowly being strangled to death. Their slow and gradual destruction is being done by ivy. The ivy is growing up the trunk and along the branches. For many years the tree survives but ultimately it dies, choked by the creeper. I saw several dead trees, the life strangled out of them by the ivy. I also noticed several that were still living, but on which the ivy was well on its way to completing its deadly work.

Covetousness is like that. Little by little it travels along the various boughs and branches of our lives until in the end it masters us. As our Lord himself said: *You cannot serve God and mammon.* And, *It is easier for a camel to go through the eye of a needle than for a rich man to enter the kingdom of*

God (Matt. 6:24; Mark 10:25).

Next to the parable of the Prodigal Son, perhaps the best-known parable is that of The Sower. You may remember how as the farmer sowed the seed, some fell into places where thorns grew up and choked the corn. The Lord gave us the interpretation of the parable (Mark 4:3-20). The thorns stand for covetousness. What is covetousness if not that desire for more things which competes against our desire for God until it wins and strangles the desire for God in our souls?

Is it not surely tragic that 'mod cons', or furniture, or holidays, or cars, or shares, or money in the bank, should strangle the life of God in the soul of a man or woman? Yet the desire for possessions stalks through our lives as the great competitor to the word of God. Possessions can crowd out the Lord until the One who is our Maker, our God, is squeezed out altogether, as the deadly creeper of covetousness takes over.

You see, Almighty God will not put up with contempt for his grace. So he quietly leaves us to our trash. Mark you! not before he has often spoken to us, called us, and rebuked us again and again. He does not leave us until he has lovingly and faithfully challenged us and shown us the stupidity and viciousness of our selfishness and greed. He will not depart until he has often shone into our hearts by the light of his word to reveal to us our folly and sin in refusing to let go of our covetousness.

Nevertheless, when he is ignored and spurned

repeatedly, the Lord sadly departs. Though we may continue to go through all the motions of our religion, and pose as fine folk, the truth is that written over the door of our hearts is the word, 'Ichabod', which means, 'The glory of the Lord has departed'. That is the final curse of covetousness, of those secret, hidden desires of selfish greed, which we cherish and indulge. They choke forever the voice of Christ, and cast us out into the hell of eternal separation from God. That is the danger of covetousness! It's as deadly as that.

Eternal security
The question arises in the light of what I have just said as to whether this means that a person can actually lose their salvation through covetousness. Such a possibility must not be taken as an implication of the teaching on covetousness found in the parable of The Sower. For those in the condition of Saul before he came to faith in Christ, as yet they have not been blessed with the saving grace of God. There is therefore no grace to lose! For those who have been born again, the 'withdrawal' from them of the Holy Spirit (Ps. 51:11), must not be understood as the loss of their salvation, but rather as the loss of assurance, fruitfulness and God's gracious blessing.

Believers may not presume on the grace of God. Disobedience on the part of a Christian – and persistent covetousness is just one example of such disobedience to the known will of God for his children – will invariably lead to a loss of grace in a relative sense, though not in the sense of losing eternal security.

It must be emphasised that the biblical teaching on the eternal security of the believer may not be misused to give a false sense of security. God still disciplines his children. When we persist in disobeying him, the results for us can be quite devastating. His love is tough enough to bring stinging strokes of his chastening rod upon our backs. Our modern sentimentality over discipline of children is a far cry from the reality of our God. In his holiness and righteousness, he may not spare us every grievous sorrow and suffering, all because he loves us and will not allow us to destroy ourselves by our rebellion against his will for us. This is why there is no contradiction between Peter's exhortation to us to fear God and John's assurance that perfect love casts out fear (1 Pet. 2:17; 1 John 4:18).

The cure for covetousness

After the rich young ruler left and Jesus had said, *It is easier for a camel to go through the eye of a needle than for a rich man to enter the kingdom of God,* the disciples asked in amazement, *Who then can be saved?* Dramatically demonstrated before them had been the impossibility of earning one's way to heaven by keeping the Ten Commandments. It had been a crystal clear object lesson. Try as hard as we may, live as good a life as we can, we may never use the Ten Commandments as a ladder to heaven. That is why the disciples said in effect, 'It is impossible then, no one can ever make it!' But Jesus replied: *With man this is impossible, but not with God: all things are possible with God* (Mark 10:27).

When we were at school, we used to hear about lepers in bygone days who had to live as outcasts beyond the town walls. We heard how they would set up their miserable settlements a little way off from the town gates, and beg from travellers about to enter the town. Covetousness is like leprosy. It infects and defiles us. That is why we may not pass through the gates into the kingdom of heaven. As the old children's hymn has it: 'Nought that defileth, nought that defileth, can ever enter in.' How then did the Lord Jesus say that it is possible to get in?

He must do two things for us. First, he must cleanse us from our sin of covetousness. When my parents were in Congo sixty years ago, they used to take into their home little children who had been put under the witchdoctor's curse. Many of these children had for months been living rough in the jungle. They were infected with awful skin complaints, they were crawling with fleas and their hair was full of lice. The first thing that had to be done was to disinfect them. Then they could be clothed. God's work of grace is like that. He has to deal with and cleanse our covetousness along with all our sins. That is why the Lord died: it was to cleanse us.

179

The second thing God must do is to begin to work a change in our hearts from being self-centred and greedy into being God-centred and generous. For many of us that is going to be a colossal transformation. It doesn't happen overnight. It is a work of grace that takes many years. That is the great evangelical purpose of the Ten Commandments. Their first great function is to drive us to our knees, like the tax-collector in the parable who beat on his breast, and would not even lift his eyes to heaven, but prayed, *God be merciful to me, a sinner.* That man was asking God first to cleanse him, and then to change him.

As we have considered together the message of this book, carefully studying in turn each of the commandments, has it dawned on you that you have a problem? Have you at last seen the real condition of your life? Have you reached the stage of silently crying, *Lord, be merciful to me, a sinner!* Are you ready for Christ first to cleanse you, and then to begin to change you?

'How does it happen?' you may ask. When you visit your doctor because you are unwell, you tell him your symptoms. Do that with the Saviour. Tell him your symptoms. Share with him what the Ten Commandments have uncovered to you of your secret, inner condition. Then ask him to prescribe his soothing, cleansing grace and to begin the work of transplanting into you a new heart that will be generous and filled with love of him.

'Will that be the end of my covetousness?'

someone asks. No it will not. But it will be the beginning of a new life in which new attitudes and new values begin to challenge and resist the old attitudes and desires. Read the Sermon on the Mount in Matthew 6 where Jesus says, *Seek first the Kingdom of God and His righteousness, and all the other things will be added to you* (Matt. 6:33). Instead of your desires being riveted on fleeting possessions, your eyes will be on the Lord. Instead of living for things that we will leave behind us when we die, we will begin to live for God, trusting him for all our needs.

Begin also to take an intelligent and informed interest in the needs of others in this sad old world. Find out about the work of missionary societies and organisations such as TEAR Fund. Learn of the desperate plight of men and women, boys and girls, who own literally nothing except the rags in which they are half-clothed, many of whom are dying in poverty and squalor. Direct some of the goods and money God has entrusted to you towards helping them. Start stewarding your money carefully and prayerfully. To do this will be a helpful antidote to greed and covetousness.

The woman meets an old boyfriend. She says to him, 'Our friendship was in the past. It is all finished. I am married now. I have two children and I dearly love my husband.' The former 'flame' is firmly turned away. The Christian meets the old covetous greed and self-centred, grasping spirit that once held him in its deadly power, and he says, 'I

181

belong to Christ now. I live for him. More, I love him and I am in his family.' It is not that the Christian doesn't enjoy the material things of this life. Rather is it that the Christian realises that he is a steward, a manager of these things. They don't belong to us. They are only on loan. Ours is the work of using them well and wisely and that includes, most importantly of all, using them for God and his kingdom.

My old associate minister in my previous congregation often quoted Paul's words to Timothy. Paul, who as Saul of Tarsus had such a struggle with covetousness, who had so loved his wealth and had his heart fixed on his money and possessions, this same Paul as an old man wrote: *Godliness with contentment is great gain!* (1 Tim. 6:6). That is the secret of living – to be content. Content because our lives belong to Christ, and he belongs to us. Content because we know one day we will be with him forever. Content because we are glad and eager to share with others what little God entrusts to us.

Our Lord had no house. No bank account. No wardrobe. No antiques. No valuable ornaments. But he was a perfect Man, completely fulfilled, always gracious, ever in touch with God. He coveted no one's goods or money. It is this Jesus Christ who says to you and me: *You shall not covet!*

Study Guide

Chapter One:
Introduction to the Ten Commandments

1. Discuss what Paul meant by the phrase 'Christ is the end of the law' (Rom. 10:4).

2. In what three ways does the Old Testament appear to set the Ten Commandments apart from the rest of the levitical law, ceremonial and civil? What are the implications of this for the Christian today?

3. How is it that we can speak of the 'grace of law'? 'Do this and *earn* life' would be legalism. What is legalism and why does it have no place in the Christian gospel?

4. Jesus said the greatest commandment is to love God. How is this fulfilled in terms of the Ten Commandments?

5. The second greatest commandment is to love our neighbours as ourselves. How does this work out today in terms of the Ten Commandments?

6. In what way are the Ten Commandments an expression of the Triune God?

Chapter Two:
The First Commandment, No False Gods

1. Discuss the meaning of the phrase 'the image of God' (see Gen. 1:26-27; Eph. 4:24). How might John 1:4, 9 have some bearing on the meaning? Read the context of 1 Corinthians 15:49 and discuss what 'the image of God' might mean for believers in the future.

2. Discuss what might be other gods in the lives of the people in your neighbourhood and what could easily

become another god for members of your church? Have you already some other god you worship?

3. 'Man's chief end is to glorify God and enjoy him forever.' What prevents us from enjoying the Lord our God?

4. What do the Ten Commandments tell us about God's love for his people?

5. What is the relationship between redemption and the commandments of God?

6. Discuss the importance of keeping the balance between the divine imminence (God's loving nearness to us) and the divine transcendence (God's awesome holiness). See 1 John 4:16 and Hebrews 12:28-29.

Chapter Three
The Second Commandment, True and False Worship

1. Explore ways in which we can dishonour God by reducing him to 'a very ordinary Wizard of Oz'.

2. Discuss ways in which worship of the creature instead of the Creator can lead to the destruction of both mind and body.

3. What distractions in your worship of God do you sometimes experience? How can we keep our attention focused on God in our worship?

4. 'God's jealousy speaks of the exclusiveness of God's love' (p.41). How can Christians today be unfaithful to God and stir up his jealousy? What practical, harmful consequences of such infidelity are there for daily Christian living?

5. This commandment contains God's word to parents. How should this be understood and applied today?

6. How can children and young people show respect for their parents and yet avoid imitating family sins? How can the church fellowship help in this dilemma?

Chapter Four
The Third Commandment, Honouring God's Name

1. Discuss the distinction between reverence for the many names of God and reverence for what the name stands for – the Person of God. When there are so many different names for God, what is the important link between the name and the Person?

2. One day we praise the Lord, the next we curse or miscall his creatures. Are there any ways in which we can discipline ourselves not to fall habitually into this sin?

3. 'Outward obedience – inward disobedience' (p.54). Discuss insincerity in the worship of God which involves merely going through the motions. Make a list of those things which can rob worship of true spirituality.

4. Is it possible for a genuine believer to despise Christ's sacrifice for sin (Heb. 10:29)? If you think that it is, then discuss what you understand 'trampling the Son of God underfoot' to mean and suggest how believers can avoid this serious sin.

5. How can we discern if an apparent work of God is genuine or not and so avoid coming close to denying the work of the Holy Spirit?

6. Say how you think we can share in the work of enabling God's name to be hallowed.

Chapter Five
The Fourth Commandment, The Sabbath Day

1. Give examples of ways in which our Lord's Day observance can become legalistic.

2. Discuss the practice of being still and quiet. Can you suggest any ways of encouraging Sabbath 'ceasing' in your family and personal life?

3. Suggest practical measures parents could take to make the Lord's Day a delight for their children rather than a bore!

4. How would you keep one day in seven special as a day of rest and worship if you lived in a non-Christian culture where the practice was to work seven days every week? How do you think the Christians of the first few centuries honoured the Lord's Day in a pagan culture? (Some background work might be needed for this question.)

5. Sabbath in the Old Testament was a celebration of *creation* – God's work. Can New Testament believers like ourselves celebrate creation and, if so, how?

6. New Testament believers met on the first day of the week because it was on that day the Risen Christ had first appeared to them. What are the implications of that for our worship and rest on the first day of the week?

Chapter Six
The Fifth Commandment, Honouring our parents

1. What theological reasons can you think of for the first commandment of the 'Second Table' being directed to our attitudes to parents rather than to the disadvantaged and destitute? Does this tell us something about the family unit and the man and woman being created in the divine image?

2. What counsel would you give to a young Christian whose parents had forbidden him or her to attend church or meet with other Christians?

3. What counsel might be given to parents to enable them to encourage loving obedience in the home on the part of their children?

4. Are there any ways in which the attitudes of believers towards frail, elderly parents will differ markedly from the attitudes of unbelievers? How can younger people show respect for the elderly?

5. We are enjoined to respect and obey our elders for their work's sake (Heb. 13:17; 1 Pet. 5:5). What aspects of their work and office in the church (see Acts 20:28-31; 1 Pet. 5:1-4) call for our respect?

6. Discuss the implication of the fifth commandment for both employers and employees.

7. How does the example of Jesus both in his family life and in his ministry help us to realise the implications of this commandment (Lk. 2:48-52; Mk. 3:31-35; Jn. 2:4; 19:26-27)?

Chapter Seven
The Sixth Commandment, No murder

1. How must a Christian handle the desire for revenge when, say, a relative or close friend has been seriously injured or murdered? (see Rom. 12:19.)

2. The clash of different cultures within the same community (e.g. Afro-Asian and Western cultures) can very easily lead to racial tension and a subsequent ghetto mentality. How can Christians give a lead in a community to enable families from very different backgrounds to live together in harmony and love?

3. Does this sixth commandment have a word to say to those who would use violent means – even murder – to oppose evils such as abortion? Discuss.

4. While most would agree it is the duty of the state to defend the lives and liberty of its citizens (Rom. 13:1ff.), what should the attitude of Christians be when the state fails in its duty and the church is unjustly harried and persecuted? (See 1 Pet. 2:13-25; Rev. 6:9-11; 7:13-14; 12:10-11.)

5. Do you agree or disagree with the author's view that the Old Testament law on capital punishment (Gen. 9:6) is not revoked in the New Testament (Rom. 13:1-4)? Give reasons for your answers

6. Caring people will 'care by being courteous road users, driving with consideration for others, because the motor car in irresponsible hands can be a violent killer' (p.109). In what other practical ways can Christians be caring people and so fulfil the spirit of this commandment?

Chapter Eight
The Seventh Commandment, Marriage

1. The author claims love has become a quest for self-fulfilment. Discuss the true meaning of love in contrast to this popular contemporary view. (See Eph. 5:21-31.)

2. Do you agree that in our 21st century culture, stable Christian marriages must be a vital aspect of the church's witness to Jesus Christ? If so, how can we guard and keep marriage relationships faithful to the glory of God?

3. What practical ways are there in which we can ensure that the false attitudes of a godless society do not encroach upon and ensnare Christian families?

4. Turn to 1 Corinthians 6:12-20 and study the three statements beginning, 'Do you not know ...?' (vs. 15,

16, 19). What is Paul asserting in each of these questions and why?

5. What is the answer to the argument which says, 'Sex is only natural so indulge yourself'? (See 1 Cor. 6:13-14.)

6. List the four defences the author suggests believers can use to be strengthened in their resolve to avoid immorality (pp.125-130). Discuss each of these and consider how each defensive position can be (a) dangerously weakened and (b) graciously strengthened.

7. The New Testament *commands* Christians to love their marriage partners. In what ways does this view of love differ from the sentimental worldly idea of 'falling in love'?

Chapter Nine
The Eighth Commandment, No Theft

1. In what thoughtless ways can employees (even Christians) steal unwittingly from their employers.

2. Discuss the section in this chapter on *Dealings in the business world* (pp.136ff.) and suggest other ways in which dishonesty is practised and even accepted as the norm in everyday life.

3. How do the nation's bankruptcy laws stand beside the laws God gave to his people in the Old Testament days? Are our contemporary laws both just and compassionate?

4. Is the principle of restitution still valid today? In what kind of circumstances would it be appropriate and right for you to make restitution to a neighbour, friend or workmate?

5. Discuss the charge brought against the people by the prophet that they had been robbing God (Mal. 3:88ff.).

6. Discuss the differences between a false 'prosperity theology' that teaches God's will is for all believers to be wealthy, and the Bible's faithful promises that God is never anyone's debtor. (See Malachi 3:10ff.)

Chapter Ten
The Ninth Commandment

1. 'How can you have a meaningful relationship with a liar?' (p.153). What ways are there in which we are economical with the truth' or guilty of 'terminological inexactitudes' – in other words, do we call our withholding of the truth by other names to conceal from ourselves our dishonesty?

2. Are there any practical ways in which the integrity of a nation (with a waning Christian heritage) can be maintained so that honesty remains a cornerstone of that society?

3. 'Is it kind? Is it true? Is it necessary?' (p.156). Discuss this criterion as a possible standard for conversations at social evenings. In what ways, if any, might such a criterion change the course of some socialising?

4. Is James exaggerating when he states that no one can tame the tongue (Jas. 3:8)? Share ways in which we can work at controlling this unruly member of our bodies.

5. David prayed for truth to permeate his inner being (Ps. 51:6). Since this is the desire of God for his people, should Christians not regularly echo that same prayer? Discuss the effect such a prayer, fervently prayed, might have in your congregation.

6. Jesus said, 'I am the truth' (Jn. 14:6) and John wrote that 'God is light' (1 Jn. 1:5). What need might there be for inner truth in your home congregation and how could this attribute of God be linked with the work of the Holy

Spirit (who is the Spirit of truth) empowering and blessing the church?

Chapter Eleven
The Tenth Commandment, Covetousness

1. Discuss how covetousness is linked to crime.

2. Paul writes, 'Sin revived and I died' (Rom. 7:9). In what ways does our discovery of covetousness and greed in our hearts reveal to us the true depths of sin within?

3. Why does Paul say that the very commandment which slew him is 'holy, just and good' (Rom. 7:12)?

4. How might the church have lost her cutting edge because she has lost the simplicity of the counter culture Jesus commends to us in the Sermon on the Mount (Matt. 6:19-34)? Do we believe and therefore practise the ideals offered to us by the Lord in this teaching?

5. What is the cure of covetousness? How can you enlarge on what is suggested in the book?

6. How does the teaching of Jesus in Luke 16:9-15 help us in our relationship with the material things of life with which God may have blessed us? (N.B. In Luke 16:10ff., 'very little' refers to material things while 'much' refers to spiritual growth and maturity. 'Worldly wealth' NIV (lit. 'unrighteous mammon' AV, RSV) is parallel to 'very little' and refers to what is temporarily entrusted to us to steward for God's glory and kingdom. '... true riches' is parallel to 'much', and refers again to spiritual growth and maturity. Parallel to 'very little' and 'worldly wealth' is 'that which is another's' because money and goods are only fleetingly on loan to us for the duration of our short lives. '... that which is your own' is parallel to 'much' and 'true riches' because spiritual maturity – for example, our likeness to the Saviour – will stay with us throughout all eternity.)

Also published by Christian Focus

Be Strong in the Lord
David Searle

An exposition of Paul's description of the
Christian's spiritual armour in Ephesians 6.

ISBN 1-85792-143-7   192 pages

**Published by Christian Focus
and Rutherford House**

Coming Alive
Jeremy Middleton
A ten-part course to explain
the basics of the Christian Faith
ISBN 094 606 871 2

Staying Alive
Jeremy Middleton
A twelve-part course for
discipling new believers
ISBN 094 606 879 8